OCR GCSE (9-1)

MEDIA STUDIES
TEACHER GUIDE

Susan Dickinson • James Guest • Eileen Lewis
Rebecca Morris • Michael Rodgers

HODDER
EDUCATION
AN HACHETTE UK COMPANY

CONTENTS

Although every effort has been made to ensure that website addresses are correct at time of going to press, Hodder Education cannot be held responsible for the content of any website mentioned. It is sometimes possible to find a relocated web page by typing in the address of the home page for a website in the URL window of your browser.

Orders: please contact Bookpoint Ltd, 130 Milton Park, Abingdon, Oxon OX14 4SB. Telephone: (44) 01235 827720. Fax: (44) 01235 400454. Lines are open 9.00–17.00, Monday to Saturday, with a 24-hour message answering service.
Visit our website at www.hoddereducation.co.uk

ISBN 978 1 5104 3516 2

© Susan Dickinson, James Guest, Eileen Lewis, Rebecca Morris, Michael Rodgers 2018

First published in 2018 by

Hodder Education

An Hachette UK Company,

Carmelite House, 50 Victoria Embankment

London EC4Y 0DZ

Impression number   10 9 8 7 6 5 4 3 2 1

Year   2022 2021 2020 2019 2018

Illustrations by Barking Dog

Typeset in Din Regular 11/13pt by Integra Software Services Pvt. Ltd., Pondicherry, India

Printed in the UK by Hobbs the Printers Ltd

A catalogue record for this title is available from the British Library

MIX
Paper from
responsible sources
FSC™ C104740

How to use these resources

These 'Approaches to teaching' have been designed to correspond with the Scheme of Work. However, each section has been designed to work independently so that teachers can adapt it to fit in with their own Scheme of Work if so desired.

We have ensured that the Scheme of Work and the Approaches are available in Word (as well as PDFs) so that teachers can use them as a starting point and adapt them to fit their own plans and their learners' needs, as appropriate.

Structure of the Scheme of Work

Year 1

The course begins with five introductory weeks covering the nine media forms, the theoretical framework, Media Language, Media Representations and Media Audiences.

Six weeks are then devoted to work on music videos and music magazines for Section A of J200/02, followed by three introductory weeks on *Cuffs* for Television Crime Drama (Section A of J200/01).

Two weeks are spent introducing Promoting Media for Section B of J200/01 by studying advertising for *The Lego Movie.*

Two further weeks focus on an introduction to online, social and participatory media, by studying *The Observer* homepage, Instagram and Twitter feed for Section B of J200/02.

These introductory weeks focus on Media Language and Representation in print, audio-visual and online products and have been included here so that learners have a good grounding for their production work for the NEA later in the year.

The remaining weeks in Year 1 are devoted to the NEA (J200/03/04): the production of a media product with a particular representation that appeals to a specific audience. The work begins with a preliminary production to familiarise learners with the equipment and to develop the necessary production skills. Learners' research and planning are carefully guided by the teacher, as is the writing of the Statement of Intent. Interim guidelines with peer assessment are identified in order to support learners in meeting the deadline for the final submission.

Year 2

NB In Year 2, where learners revisit areas they have looked at in Year 1, contexts are investigated and explored (these are not covered in Year 1).

Learners begin Year 2 by completing their study of Promoting Media for Section B of J200/01 in the first five weeks. They revisit the work done in Year 1 on *The Lego Movie* advertising, investigating the institutional background to Time Warner and *The Lego Movie Video Game.*

Learners revisit the work on *Cuffs* for three weeks and then work for four weeks on *The Avengers*, investigating social and cultural contexts, genre and audience appeal for Television (Section A of J200/01). Five weeks are then spent developing learners' knowledge and understanding of radio, music videos and music magazines.

The final eight weeks of teaching are spent on News for Section B of J200/02. *The Observer* is studied in terms of institution, regulation, funding and audience. Three historical versions of *The Observer* are studied, comparing them with contemporary editions in terms of changes in social, cultural and political contexts. This work finishes with a comparison between *The Observer* online, its Twitter and Instagram feeds and its print counterpart.

The course concludes with five weeks devoted to revision for each section of the exams J200/01 and J200/02.

Key changes

For teachers who are using OCR's GCSE in Media Studies (J526), these are the key differences between the legacy specification and the GCSE (9–1) in Media Studies (J200).

Media Studies GCSE J526	Media Studies GCSE (9–1) J200
One exam (1 hour 45 minutes) with an unseen extract (choice of moving image or print). Centres able to choose their own comedy texts for Section B of the exam on scheduling and audiences.	Two exams, worth 35% each: one with a moving image extract from one of two set products, which have been studied by learners. J200/01 contains one in-depth study of television and the study of other set products. J200/02 includes one in-depth study of magazines and one in-depth study of online, social and participatory media, together with the study of other set products.
Key concepts (media language, representation, institutions, audience) underpin the study of media **texts**.	**The theoretical framework** (media language, media representations, media industries and media audiences) underpins the study of media **products**. Contexts and theoretical perspectives, such as Blumler and Katz's uses and gratifications theory and Propp's narrative theory, must also be studied.
Three media forms must be studied in the course as a whole: print, audio-visual and online.	**Nine** media forms must be studied in the course as a whole: television; film; radio; newspapers; magazines; advertising and marketing; online, social and participatory media; video games; and music video.
Two controlled assessment portfolios, worth 30% each.	One non-examined assessment component, worth 30%.
The production portfolio is assessed in three sections: research and planning, production, evaluation.	Only the production itself is assessed, although a Statement of Intent must be included with the work.
A choice of 12 briefs published in the specification.	A choice of four briefs with a specified audience and genre, released on 1 March of Year 1 of the course (briefs change every year).
Learners can work individually or in groups of up to five.	The NEA production must be individual, but learners can use unassessed learners as crew.

Year 1

Week	Component(s) Media form(s) Set product(s)	Aims/Area of framework	Learning objectives Learners will be able to:	Activities	Assessment/Homework
1	All	Induction Introduction to media forms Introduction to the theoretical framework	• Identify the nine media forms • Reflect on their own consumption/use of media products • Understand the structure of the GCSE course • State the four areas of the theoretical framework • Apply one of the four areas of the theoretical framework to a media product	Ice-breakers Invent acronyms, e.g. 'LAIR' for the framework, 'VT MAN FORM' for the media forms Discuss significance and influence of the nine media forms Apply the theoretical framework to a media product	**Homework:** Name three products in three different media forms which they particularly enjoy and explain why. Select one film poster and annotate it, using one area of the theoretical framework.
2	C1/C2/C3 Newspapers Magazines Online	**Introduction to media language** for print and online products	• Analyse examples of layout, typography, language use, use of images, graphics and colour • Suggest connotations for examples of media language use • Analyse the ways in which media producers use media language to create meanings for audiences • Analyse the ways in which media producers use contrasting media language to address their audiences	Analyse a range of print and online products exemplifying different styles of media language	Assess: • ability to distinguish between different styles of media language • ability to suggest different connotations for these different styles **Homework:** Write up an analysis of a print or online product. Make collages of contrasting media language.

Week	Component(s) Media form(s) Set product(s)	Aims/Area of framework	Learning objectives Learners will be able to:	Activities	Assessment/Homework
3	C1/C2/C3 Television Music videos	**Introduction to media language** for audio-visual products	● Analyse examples of camerawork, editing, mise-en-scène and soundtrack ● Suggest connotations for examples of media language use ● Recognise generic conventions of crime drama	Analyse a range of television products exemplifying different styles of media language	Assess: ● ability to distinguish between different styles of media language ● ability to suggest different connotations for these different styles **Homework:** Log types of media language use in different types of television programme, e.g. news, soap, prime-time drama, reality TV. Write up an analysis of one of the key elements of media language in a TV crime drama extract.
4	C1/C2/C3 Music videos Advertising and marketing (A&M)	**Introduction to media representations**	● State how media producers have chosen to select representational elements and not select others ● Analyse gender stereotypes in music videos and advertising ● Suggest how the construction of reality in music videos and advertising might fit the producers' purposes	Explore presence and absence (e.g. of gender, race/ethnicity, disability, age) in a range of products Analyse examples of heavily gender stereotyped music videos and advertisements and link these to promotion of the brand	Assess: ● ability to explain selection of representations in terms of the producers' purposes ● ability to recognise gender stereotypes **Homework:** Produce a mock-up for a CD front cover for a new artist, with an anti-stereotypical representation of gender. Collect examples of anti-stereotyping in ads and videos.

					Assess:

| 5 | C1/C2/C3
TV
Radio
Music videos
Video games
Online | **Introduction to media audiences** | • State examples of television and radio channels with mass and niche audiences

• Discuss how audiences may be passive and/or active in a range of media forms: television, radio, music videos, magazines, video games and online/participatory media | Use TV and radio schedules to suggest target audiences to give examples of mass and niche audiences (e.g. BBC1 and BBC4, Radio 2 and Radio 3)

Discuss how to arrange the media forms on a continuum from active to passive | Assess:
• ability to distinguish between mass and niche audiences
• ability to explain audience activity and passivity
Homework:
Log own media use over one day and evaluate its activity/passivity. Research a news story or television/radio programme which has provoked contrasting audience responses. |
| 6 | C2/C3
Music videos | Introduction to music videos: to explore how different videos from different musical genres use **media language** and **representations** to differentiate the musical artist | • Compare and contrast the media language styles of music videos from different musical genres
• State the codes and conventions of the music video as a media form
• Analyse how music videos use media language to create connotations that fit the artists' images
• Analyse how music videos use representations to fit the artists' images
• Discuss which social groups are under-represented or misrepresented in music videos | View videos from a range of popular music genres and discuss how the style fits the genre and the artist

Analyse what the videos have in common – e.g. mostly non-diegetic sound, fast-paced editing, energetic camerawork, performance to camera, narrative driven by performance by a fictional narrative

Discuss which social groups are under-represented (e.g. people with disabilities) or misrepresented (e.g. objectification of women) in music videos | Assess:
• ability to analyse how different representations and styles of media language fit different artists
• ability to state the codes and conventions of the music video form
• ability to exemplify absence and misrepresentation
Homework:
Write up the media language analysis of one of the music videos from lesson.
View at least three videos from genres with which you are not familiar and log whether or not they fit the conventions of music videos as a form. |

Scheme of Work

Week	Component(s) Media form(s) Set product(s)	Aims/Area of framework	Learning objectives Learners will be able to:	Activities	Assessment/Homework
7	C2/C3 Music videos Chosen products	Set music videos: to analyse the similarities and differences in **media language**	● Compare and contrast the camerawork in the two chosen videos ● Compare and contrast editing in the two chosen videos ● Compare and contrast the use of mise-en-scène in the two chosen videos ● Compare and contrast the use (if any) of diegetic sound in the two chosen videos ● State any use of intertextuality in the chosen videos	In-depth analysis of the two music videos	Assess: ● ability to accurately use technical terms ● ability to compare and contrast media language elements and their connotations **Homework:** Write up the camerawork and editing analysis of set music videos from lesson. Essay: 'How do the two music videos you have studied use media language in the same way and differently?'
8	C2/C3 Music videos Chosen products	Set music videos: to analyse **media representations** in the set music videos	● Compare and contrast the social groups represented in the two chosen videos ● Compare and contrast the use of stereotypes (or anti-stereotypes) in the two chosen videos ● Compare and contrast the messages and values in the two chosen videos	In-depth analysis of the two music videos	Assess: ● ability to explain how different social groups are represented or the same group is represented differently or similarly ● ability to explain similarities or differences in stereotyping ● understanding of the underlying messages and values, e.g. what is being celebrated or criticised in the videos, and how these are shared by other media products **Homework:** Write up the media representation analysis of set music videos from lesson. View other videos by the same artists.

9	C2/C3 Music magazines	Introduction to music magazines: to explore magazine **media language** and generic conventions	• State the codes and conventions of the magazine as a media form • Compare and contrast the media language styles of music magazines from different musical genres • State the generic codes and conventions of the music magazine	View a variety of magazine front covers from different genres (e.g. current affairs, lifestyle, special interest) and list the codes of the magazine as a form: masthead, cover lines, cover image, etc. View at least three music magazine front covers and list generic conventions, e.g. image of musician(s) on front cover, addressing fandom for a musical genre, the tone of the magazine matches that of the genre of music	Assess: • ability to state the codes and conventions of the magazine as a media form • ability to state the specific codes and conventions of the music magazine genre **Homework:** Write up the media language analysis of one of the magazines from lesson. Essay: 'Write an analysis of one of the front covers discussed in class, using the correct media terminology.'
10	C2/C3 Music magazines *MOJO*	Set music magazine: to analyse the use of **media language** in *MOJO* to address its target **audience**	• Analyse *MOJO* front covers in terms of layout, typography, image, graphics, colour and language use • Suggest how this media language addresses a mature, mostly male audience of fans of 'classic rock' • State the main features of the house style of the whole magazine • State how two regular features in the magazine address the target audience • State any use of intertextuality in the magazine	In-depth analysis of the two front covers Comparison of the media language on the front covers with that throughout the magazine Comparison of the content across at least two issues to ascertain which are the regular features	Assess: • ability to analyse front covers in terms of media language audience address • knowledge and understanding of the content of the magazine as a whole **Homework:** Write up the media language analysis of *MOJO* magazine from lesson. Pick one other music magazine and note how the layout, typography, images and graphics, use of colour and language differ from those of *MOJO*.

Week	Component(s) Media form(s) Set product(s)	Aims/Area of framework	Learning objectives Learners will be able to:	Activities	Assessment/Homework
11	C2/C3 Music magazines *MOJO*	Set music magazine: to analyse **representations** in *MOJO* and discuss how they address its target **audience**	<ul><li>Analyse the social groups present in and absent from *MOJO* magazine</li><li>Discuss the reasons for this presence/absence</li><li>Discuss the use of stereotypes (and/or anti-stereotypes) in *MOJO* magazine – especially gender stereotypes</li><li>Analyse the messages and values in *MOJO* magazine</li><li>Suggest how these representations address a mature, mostly male audience of fans of 'classic rock'</li></ul>	In-depth analysis of the two front covers in terms of representations Investigation into whether the content of the magazines excludes social groups based on gender, age, sexuality, race/ethnicity	Assess: <ul><li>ability to explain selection in representation</li><li>ability to explain stereotyping</li><li>understanding of the underlying messages and values, e.g. what is being celebrated or criticised in the magazine, and how these are shared by other media products</li><li>ability to link representation to audience</li></ul>**Homework:** Write up the media representation analysis of *MOJO* magazine from lesson. Pick one other music magazine and note how the representations differ from those of *MOJO*.
12	C1/C3 TV *Cuffs*	Set TV programme: to analyse crime drama genre **conventions** and **narrative** in *Cuffs*	<ul><li>State the generic codes and conventions of the crime drama</li><li>Exemplify how *Cuffs* fits crime drama codes and conventions</li><li>Analyse how *Cuffs* creates ongoing multiple storylines based on the 'everyday life' of a police station</li></ul>	Exposition: crime drama conventions Screen whole episode of *Cuffs* Discuss which conventions apply List the possible storylines established in the first episode of *Cuffs*	Assess: <ul><li>ability to exemplify crime drama conventions in *Cuffs*</li><li>ability to distinguish between series and serial narratives and explain the serial opportunities in the first episode of *Cuffs*</li><li>understanding of concept of 'social realism' in drama</li><li>ability to link serial realist narratives to television as a scheduled, domestic media form</li></ul>

		Objectives	Activities	Homework / Assess
		<ul><li>Discuss how successfully *Cuffs* creates a social realism like that of a soap opera</li><li>State how broadcast television as a technology suits serial narratives (e.g. as compared with film)</li></ul>	<ul><li>Discuss the similarities between *Cuffs* and soap opera in creating a social world that audiences will accept as 'real'</li><li>Discuss how TV scheduling relies on repeated narratives – series or serials – and give examples of each type</li></ul>	**Homework:** Watch one other crime drama and note similar or different use of conventions. Write a review of a television crime drama.
13	C1/C3 TV *Cuffs*	Set TV programme: to analyse the **media language** elements and **audience** address in key sequences from *Cuffs* <ul><li>Analyse the camerawork in sequences from *Cuffs*</li><li>Analyse the editing in sequences from *Cuffs*</li><li>Analyse the mise-en-scène in sequences from *Cuffs*</li><li>Analyse the soundtrack in sequences from *Cuffs*</li><li>State any use of intertextuality in the sequences</li></ul>	In-depth analysis of short sequences from *Cuffs*	Assess: <ul><li>ability to accurately use technical terms</li><li>ability to analyse media language elements and their connotations</li></ul>**Homework:** Research reviews of *Cuffs*.
14	C1/C3 TV *Cuffs*	Set TV programme: to analyse the **representations** and **audience** address in *Cuffs* <ul><li>Analyse the social groups present in and absent from *Cuffs*</li><li>Discuss the reasons for this presence/absence</li><li>Discuss the use of stereotypes (and/or anti-stereotypes) in *Cuffs* – especially gender stereotypes</li><li>Analyse the messages and values in *Cuffs*</li></ul>	Create a character list for the *Cuffs* episode and review for inclusion/exclusion – noting deliberate attempts at inclusion by the producers Analyse key sequences for representation	Assess: <ul><li>ability to explain selection in representation</li><li>ability to explain stereotyping</li><li>understanding of the underlying messages and values, e.g. what is being celebrated or criticised in the programme, and how these are shared by other media products</li><li>ability to link representation to a mass audience</li></ul>

Week	Component(s) Media form(s) Set product(s)	Aims/Area of framework	Learning objectives Learners will be able to:	Activities	Assessment/Homework
			• Suggest how these representations address a mainstream, pre-watershed, British mass audience	Create a narrative map of the *Cuffs* episode and discuss the messages and values communicated by these narratives Discuss how far these are mainstream messages and values that will be accepted by a mass audience including children	**Homework:** Essay: 'How do the representations and media language in *Cuffs* try to engage a mass audience?'
15	C1 A&M *The Lego Movie* posters/trailer	Set A&M: to analyse the **media language** elements in the advertising for *The Lego Movie*	• Analyse *The Lego Movie* posters in terms of layout, typography, image, graphics, colour and language use • Compare and contrast the character posters • Analyse *The Lego Movie* trailer in terms of camerawork, editing, mise-en-scène and soundtrack • Identify and analyse any use of intertextuality in *The Lego Movie* posters and trailer	In-depth analysis of the set posters In-depth analysis of the trailer	Assess: • ability to accurately use technical terms • ability to analyse media language elements and their connotations **Homework:** Select a character poster and annotate it, focusing on analysis of layout and colour. Watch some of a walkthrough for *The Lego Movie* game and prepare still shots to present to the class.

16	C1 A&M *The Lego Movie* posters/trailer	To analyse the **representations** in the advertising for *The Lego Movie*	● Analyse the social groups present in and absent from the advertising for *The Lego Movie* ● Discuss the reasons for this presence/absence ● Discuss the use of stereotypes (and/or anti-stereotypes) in the advertising for *The Lego Movie* – especially gender- and age-related stereotypes ● Analyse the messages and values in the advertising for *The Lego Movie*	Create a character list for the advertising for *The Lego Movie* and review for inclusion/exclusion Discuss why films aimed at a global market feature mostly white American characters in their advertising Discuss the anti-stereotypical representation of powerful femininity in Wyldstyle and the black (stereotypically old) sage in Vitruvius Discuss the messages about heroism, gender and social control in the advertising Discuss the differences in the trailer and poster due to opportunities offered by the different print and audio-visual technologies	Assess: ● ability to explain selection in representation ● ability to explain stereotyping ● understanding of the underlying messages and values, e.g. what is being celebrated or criticised in the advertising, and how these are shared by other media products ● ability to state two differences in the print and television adverts that reflect the technology **Homework:** Prepare a half-page essay plan on 'How far does the advertising for *The Lego Movie* use stereotypes?'. Essay: 'How far does the advertising for *The Lego Movie* use stereotypes?'
17	C2/C3 Online *The Observer*	Set online product: to analyse the **media language** elements and audience address in *The Observer* website	● Analyse *The Observer* homepage in terms of layout, typography, image, graphics, colour and language use, and links ● Suggest how this media language addresses a mixed-gender, mature, middle-class, 'progressive' audience	In-depth analysis of the homepage Exploration of pages linked from the homepage to establish the house style Discuss how two of the sections (e.g. opinion, interviews, reviews, food and lifestyle, sport) address the target audience	Assess: ● ability to analyse the homepage in terms of media language and audience address ● knowledge and understanding of the content of the website as a whole ● ability to explain how the online newspaper uses digital technology that makes it different from a print newspaper

Scheme of Work

Week	Component(s) Media form(s) Set product(s)	Aims/Area of framework	Learning objectives Learners will be able to:	Activities	Assessment/Homework
			• State the main features of the house style from the homepage that are continued through the website • State how two regular sections on the website address the target audience • State any use of intertextuality in *The Observer* website • Discuss how the online newspaper uses digital technology	Discuss what the online newspaper can do easily that the print one cannot	**Homework:** Read one opinion piece and one review, including some of the comments.
18	C2/C3 Online *The Observer*	Set online product: to analyse the **media language** elements and **audience** address in the *Guardian* Instagram and Twitter feeds	• Analyse the *Guardian* Instagram and Twitter feeds in terms of layout, typography, image, graphics, colour and language use • Suggest how this media language addresses *The Observer* target audience • State any use of intertextuality in the *Guardian* Instagram and Twitter feeds • Discuss how the Instagram and Twitter feeds use technology to allow audience participation	In-depth analysis of at least one each of the *Guardian* Instagram and Twitter feeds Discussion of how effectively *The Observer* uses these social media to encourage participation	Assess: • ability to analyse the feeds in terms of media language audience address • ability to explain how the feeds use digital technology to encourage an active audience **Homework:** Access the website for the *Mail* online and list differences from *The Observer* online.

19	C3 Magazines TV Music video Online	Preliminary production: research **representations, media language** and target **audience** in existing media products Write a short Statement of Intent	• Discuss how the practical production will use media language and representation to communicate meaning to an intended audience • Understand how individual research and planning will inform their own practical production • Understand how to write the Statement of Intent, and its significance	Individual research	Feedback on suitability of existing products used Assessment and feedback on coverage of media language, representations and audience in the short Statement of Intent **Homework:** Continue researching existing media products. Continue planning mini productions.
20	C3 Magazines TV Music video Online	Preliminary production: produce a short product	• Use technology to produce a media product • Practise and develop the relevant practical skills by creating their own individual media production • Apply their knowledge and understanding of media language and representation to express and communicate meaning to an intended audience	Production activities	**Homework:** Continue the production work.

Week	Component(s) Media form(s) Set product(s)	Aims/Area of framework	Learning objectives Learners will be able to:	Activities	Assessment/Homework
21	C3 Magazines TV Music video Online	Preliminary production: complete a short practice product; discuss what has been learned about creating productions	● Use technology to produce a media product ● Practise and develop the relevant practical skills by creating their own individual media production ● Discuss what has been learned about applying media language and representation to express and communicate meaning to an intended audience ● Learn from peers' feedback and from giving feedback to other learners	Production activities Plenary discussing what has been learned about completing productions to deadline, choosing media language style and creating representations	Assessment and feedback on the success of the product in using media language and representations to communicate meaning to an intended audience (but this is not allowed if the student is using the same product for their NEA) **Homework:** Complete the production work. Write or record a short self-evaluation of the preliminary production.
22	C3 Magazines TV Music video Online	Final production: research and planning phase To analyse how existing media products use elements of media language to create meaning, and decide whether to use similar or different strategies	● State the codes and conventions of the media form and/or the specified genre in terms of media language elements, to establish what is conventional and unconventional media language for that media form ● Understand the detailed requirements of the set briefs ● Analyse the connotations created by choice of media language in existing products	Individual research	**Homework:** Research and analyse examples of intertextuality.

		Objectives		Homework
		• Analyse how media language creates narrative, portrays aspects of reality, constructs points of view, and conveys messages and values • Investigate uses of intertextuality in existing products • State how these techniques will or will not be used in the production • Understand the importance of dates and deadlines • Understand how individual research will inform their own practical production		**Homework:** Research examples of anti-stereotypes, misrepresentations and under-represented groups.
23	C3 Magazines TV Music video Online	Final production: research and planning phase To analyse how similar existing media products create representations, and decide whether to use similar or different strategies	• Analyse the issues of stereotyping, misrepresentation or under-representation in similar media products • State how the production aims to construct representations • State how the production will use anti-stereotyping or include under-represented groups • Analyse how media language creates narrative, portrays aspects of reality, constructs points of view, and conveys messages and values	Individual research

Week	Component(s) Media form(s) Set product(s)	Aims/Area of framework	Learning objectives Learners will be able to:	Activities	Assessment/Homework
24	C3 Magazines TV Music video Online	Final production: research and planning phase To analyse how similar media products aimed at the same target audience address that audience, and decide whether to use similar or different strategies	• Discuss the style of media language that is commonly used for the target audience • Outline what may serve to alienate or patronise the target audience and what may make them feel included or flattered (e.g. effective intertextuality and conventional and/or unconventional use of media language) • Draft the Statement of Intent • State how the production aims to address the target audience • State how media language will be used to communicate meaning • State how representations will be identified and used • State how they have interpreted and responded to research findings	Individual research	**Homework:** Analyse the mode of address of a relevant media product.
25	C3 Magazines TV Music video Online	Final production: research and planning phase To plan the productions To draft the Statement of Intent	• Outline the time-line for the production • State the resources needed for the production, including use of crew • State how media language will be used to communicate meaning	Individual: • drafting of Statement of Intent • action planning	Feedback on: • suitability of locations • technical resources available • managing unassessed learners • the production schedule • health and safety

			• State how representations will be identified and used • State how the target audience will be identified, reached and addressed • State how they have interpreted and responded to research findings	**Homework:** Continue planning productions: recording planning, writing first drafts or scripts and planning layouts and storyboards.
26	C3 Magazines TV Music video Online	Final production: research and planning phase To plan the productions To complete all Statements of Intent	• Research what may serve to alienate or patronise the target audience and what may make them feel included or flattered • Reflect on how media language will be used to communicate meaning • Reflect on how representations will be identified and used • State how the target audience will be identified, reached and addressed • State how they have interpreted and responded to research findings • Understand the requirements for original footage, images and text	Individual: • completion of Statement of Intent • action planning, including use of unassessed learners Feedback on: • suitability of locations • technical resources available • managing unassessed learners • the production schedule • health and safety **Homework:** Reflect on and evaluate audience research findings and make any adjustments necessary to planned productions. Continue planning and finalising the details of the production and the production schedule.

Week	Component(s) Media form(s) Set product(s)	Aims/Area of framework	Learning objectives Learners will be able to:	Activities	Assessment/Homework
27	C3 Magazines TV Music video Online	Final production: production phase	• Prepare and present a pitch for their production to be presented to the rest of the class • State the details of how and when they intend to use crew/models/actors • State how media language will be used to communicate meaning • State how representations will be constructed • State how they intend to reach their target audience • Check their planning against their Statement of Intent	Production activities Log use of sources and unassessed learners	**Homework:** Adapt productions after reflecting on peers' responses to pitch.
28	C3 Magazines TV Music video Online	Final production: production phase	• Use technology to produce a media product • Manage the resources needed for the production, including use of crew • Use storyboards/mock-ups/drafts to produce a media product • Direct actors/models/crew in order to achieve the planned representation/s for an intended audience • Use media language to construct the planned representation/s for an intended audience	Production activities Log use of sources and unassessed learners	**Homework:** Continue working on productions, matching them against the intended audience and their Statement of Intent.

29	C3 Magazines TV Music video Online	Final production: production phase	• Use technology to produce a media product • Manage the resources needed for the production, including use of crew • Use storyboards/mock-ups/drafts to produce a media product • Direct actors/models/crew in order to achieve the planned representation/s for an intended audience • Use media language to construct the planned representation/s for an intended audience	Production activities Log use of sources and unassessed learners	**Homework:** Continue working on productions, matching them against the intended audience and their Statement of Intent.
30	C3 Magazines TV Music video Online	Final production: production phase **Interim deadline 1** Magazine/website: first page complete TV/music video: 40 seconds edited	• Use technology to produce a media product • Use media language to construct the planned representation/s for an intended audience • Edit original material to express and communicate meaning to the intended audience • Edit original material in order to construct specific representations as outlined in the Statement of Intent • Use the indicative content from the specification to produce a media product	Production activities Log use of sources and unassessed learners Self- and/or peer evaluation of the success of the first phase of the production in using media language and representations to communicate meaning to an intended audience	Feedback on: • suitability of locations • technical resources available • managing unassessed learners • the production schedule • health and safety **Homework:** Continue working on productions.

Week	Component(s) Media form(s) Set product(s)	Aims/Area of framework	Learning objectives Learners will be able to:	Activities	Assessment/Homework
31	C3 Magazines TV Music video Online	Final production: production phase	● Use technology to produce a media product ● Evaluate the success of the first phase of the production ● Write an action plan for changes needed ● Learn from peers' feedback and from giving feedback to other learners	Production activities Log use of sources and unassessed learners	**Homework:** Continue on to the second phase of productions.
32	C3 Magazines TV Music video Online	Final production: production phase	● Use technology to produce a media product ● Use media language to construct the planned representation/s for an intended audience ● Edit original material to express and communicate meaning to the intended audience ● Edit original material in order to construct specific representations as outlined in the Statement of Intent ● Use the indicative content from the specification to produce a media product	Production activities Log use of sources and unassessed learners	**Homework:** Continue working on productions.

33	C3 Magazines TV Music video Online	Final production: production phase	• Use technology to produce a media product • Use media language to construct the planned representation/s for an intended audience • Edit original material to express and communicate meaning to the intended audience • Edit original material in order to construct specific representations as outlined in the Statement of Intent • Use the indicative content from the specification to produce a media product	Production activities Log use of sources and unassessed learners	**Homework:** Continue working on productions.
34	C3 Magazines TV Music video Online	Final production: production phase **Interim deadline 2** Magazine: first two pages complete Online: first page and embedded audio or video complete TV/music video: 80 seconds edited	• Use technology to produce a media product • Use media language to construct the planned representation/s for an intended audience • Edit original material to express and communicate meaning to the intended audience • Edit original material in order to construct specific representations as outlined in the Statement of Intent • Use the indicative content from the specification to produce a media product	Production activities Log use of sources and unassessed learners Self- and/or peer evaluation of the success of the first two phases of the production in using media language and representations to communicate meaning to an intended audience	Feedback on: • suitability of locations • technical resources available • managing unassessed learners • the production schedule • health and safety **Homework:** Continue working on productions.

Scheme of Work

Week	Component(s) Media form(s) Set product(s)	Aims/Area of framework	Learning objectives Learners will be able to:	Activities	Assessment/Homework
35	C3 Magazines TV Music video Online	Final production: production phase	• Use technology to produce a media product • Evaluate the success of the second phase of the production • Write an action plan for changes needed • Learn from peers' feedback and from giving feedback to other learners	Production activities Log use of sources and unassessed learners	**Homework:** Continue on to the third phase of productions.
36	C3 Magazines TV Music video Online	Final production: production phase	• Use technology to produce a media product • Use media language to construct the planned representation/s for an intended audience • Edit original material to express and communicate meaning to the intended audience • Edit original material in order to construct specific representations as outlined in the Statement of Intent • Use the indicative content from the specification to produce a media product	Production activities Log use of sources and unassessed learners	**Homework:** Continue working on productions.
37	C3 Magazines TV Music video Online	Final production: production phase	• Use technology to produce a media product	Production activities Log use of sources and unassessed learners	**Homework:** Continue working on productions.

38	C3 Magazines TV Music video Online	Final production: production phase **Final deadline** Magazine: three pages complete Online: two pages and embedded audio or video complete TV/music video: 120 seconds edited	• Use technology to produce a media product • Use media language to construct the planned representation/s for an intended audience • Edit original material to express and communicate meaning to the intended audience • Edit original material in order to construct specific representations as outlined in the Statement of Intent • Use the indicative content from the specification to produce a media product	Production activities Log use of sources and unassessed learners	**Homework:** Continue working on productions.
39	C3 Magazines TV Music video Online	Final production: peer review of productions	• Use technology to produce a media product • Discuss and evaluate what has been learned about applying media language and representation to express and communicate meaning to an intended audience • Learn from and act on peers' feedback and from giving feedback to other learners • Action plan any further work needed on the production before the final submission	Peer review of the success of the production in using media language and representations to communicate meaning to an intended audience Action plan any further work that needs completion (under teacher supervision in additional catch-up sessions) Completion of cover sheets – reference all sources used in the production and use of unassessed learners	**Homework:** Complete the production work, making any necessary final improvements.

Year 2

Week	Component(s) Media form(s) Set product(s)	Aims/Area of framework	Learning objectives Learners will be able to:	Activities	Assessment/Homework
1	C1/C2 Film	**Introduction to media industries:** to explore Warner Bros and *The Lego Movie/The Lego Movie* video game as a case study	• Define the terms 'media conglomerate', 'vertical integration', 'diversification', 'convergence' • Exemplify the above terms using Warner Bros and *The Lego Movie/The Lego Movie* video game as a case study • Explain the role of the BBFC in regulating film in the UK	Exposition and games to test understanding of the key terms and the role of the BBFC Research Time Warner as a media conglomerate and list the media in which it competes Discuss why Time Warner has diversified into video games and how this is an example of vertical integration	Assess: • ability to define and exemplify key terms • knowledge and understanding of Time Warner as a conglomerate • understanding of the role of the BBFC **Homework:** Research box office takings by studio on www.boxofficemojo.com to compare Warner Bros with the other American studios. Using www.bbfc.co.uk as the source of information, prepare a 5–10-slide presentation about film regulation in the UK.

2	C1 A&M *The Lego Movie* posters	To review **media language** and **representations** in *The Lego Movie* posters in relation to social and cultural **contexts**, targeting **audiences** and different audience interpretations	• Explain the influence of the cultural supremacy of comic book franchises in Hollywood film production • Explain the influence of commercially and critically successful multi-layered films aimed at children and adults (e.g. *Toy Story*) on Hollywood film production • Explain the influence of 'popular feminism' within a patriarchal industry on women's roles in action films • Explain how the media language and representations in the advertising target a mass audience • Explore different possible audience interpretations of the advertising campaign (e.g. enthusiastic, unengaged, oppositional) and possible reasons for these	Review previous analysis of media language and representations in the posters Introduce the concept of 'contexts' (primarily through examples) Name some Hollywood blockbusters that are based on comic books Discuss what a franchise is and why they are used by Hollywood to reduce risk Discuss the influence of successful films like *Toy Story* that created narratives with adult themes (e.g. alienation and abandonment) that address children Discuss the influence of action heroines in recent children's cinema on *The Lego Movie*'s characters Analyse the advertising for mainstream pleasures that address a mass audience, e.g. comedy, easily identifiable characters, spectacle Discuss any differences in responses within the class group and possible reasons for these	Assess: • understanding of the range of media contexts (social, cultural, political, historical) • ability to exemplify the influence of social and cultural contexts on the advertising for *The Lego Movie* • understanding of how the media language and representations in the advertising target a mass audience • ability to state the reasons for different possible audience interpretations **Homework:** Research franchises on Box Office Mojo and Blockbuster on Wikipedia. Compare the representation of Wyldstyle with another female action heroine from the advertising for a film of their choice.

Week	Component(s) Media form(s) Set product(s)	Aims/Area of framework	Learning objectives Learners will be able to:	Activities	Assessment/Homework
3	C1 A&M *The Lego Movie* trailer	To review **media language, representations** and **audience** address in *The Lego Movie* TV trailer and all-Lego ad break To explore **media industries** in relation to the advertising and marketing of *The Lego Movie*	● Outline how the media language and representations in the TV trailer target a mass family audience ● Explain the funding of Hollywood studios, including the role of merchandising ● Explain the role of marketing in Hollywood blockbusters ● Explain the synergy that led to other companies producing television advertising that also promoted *The Lego Movie*	Review previous analysis of media language and representations in the TV ad break Exposition: the funding of films through box office, TV sales, product placement, merchandising, DVD sales and streaming rights, etc. Discuss how to get a film noticed in the six weeks leading up to its release Discuss the benefit in free promotion for *The Lego Movie* of other companies making Lego versions of their adverts, and the benefit from association with a prestige media product that these other companies hoped to achieve	Assess: ● understanding of Hollywood as a media industry, and film promotion as specialist advertising and marketing ● understanding of the role of film-related branded merchandising in creating value for the Lego brand and the film **Homework:** Research the marketing for one recent Hollywood blockbuster film. Compile a folder for *The Lego Movie* case study, ensuring that all work and notes are collated for future reference.

4 C1 Video games	To explore video games in relation to **media industries** and **audience**	• Explain the uses and gratifications offered by video games • State the role of technology in audience consumption of video games • State how games companies market games to target audiences • Identify the role of the Games Rating Authority in regulating video games • State how PEGI ratings categorise audiences	Exposition: introduction to uses and gratifications theory Discussion: what uses and gratifications the class get from video games Share knowledge on video gaming technology and audience consumption Discuss how different genres of games, e.g. first-person shooter and sports, match 3 and farm/family simulations, are aimed at different audiences by age and gender Exposition: the Games Rating Authority and PEGI ratings	Assess: • understanding of uses and gratifications theory • ability to state three uses and gratifications of video games • ability to state two or more examples of video games targeted at different audiences • identification of the Games Rating Authority and PEGI ratings **Homework:** Watch some of another walkthrough for *The Lego Movie* video game. Visit the Games Rating Authority website. Create a document that depicts the categories of audience defined by the PEGI rating system. Include acceptable content for each rating.

Week	Component(s) Media form(s) Set product(s)	Aims/Area of framework	Learning objectives Learners will be able to:	Activities	Assessment/Homework
5	C1 Video games *The Lego Movie* video game	To analyse *The Lego Movie* video game in terms of **audience** and **media language** (use of intertextuality only) Explore the influence of social/cultural **contexts** Investigate the media **industry** behind the game	• Explain how *The Lego Movie* video game offers uses and gratifications to its audience • Explain how *The Lego Movie* video game uses intertextuality to promote the film • Discuss how audiences might interpret *The Lego Movie* video game differently and why this might be so (e.g. gender, age) • Explain the influence of the social context that audiences now accept and expect merchandising for major films • State that Time Warner is a global media conglomerate funded commercially, owned by shareholders, that uses film as a prestige product to sell convergent products	Analyse the uses and gratifications offered by *The Lego Movie* video game Discuss how the game uses extracts from the film Explore different reactions to the game within the class and suggest which age group it might best suit Discuss how far class members accept and expect merchandising such as video games for major films and whether this is now seen as an integral part of a film becoming a cultural event Review the media industry behind the game	**Homework:** Essay: 'Explain how video games offer uses and gratifications, using *The Lego Movie* video game as an example.' Visit a supermarket and conduct a mini-research project on the number and nature of products linked to major films.

| 6 | C1 Television *Cuffs* | To review the analysis of *Cuffs*

 To analyse how *Cuffs* is influenced by contemporary social and cultural **contexts** | • Analyse extracts in terms of media language and representations
 • Explain the influence of patriarchy and feminism (or post-feminism) on representations in *Cuffs*
 • Explain the influence of multiculturalism on representations in *Cuffs*
 • Explain the influence of changing attitudes to sexualities on representations in *Cuffs*
 • Explain the dominance of the crime drama in contemporary television due to its potential to explore social issues in an accessible way
 • Explain how increasing competition for television is driving the search for programmes that engage audience loyalty with serial narratives | Discuss the influence of feminism on the gender representation, and multiculturalism on the ethnic/racial representation, of police officers and criminals in *Cuffs*

 Discuss the influence of changing attitudes to sexualities on the representation of the gay police officer

 Investigate TV schedules to research the importance of the crime drama to contemporary television

 List the forms of entertainment that are competing with mainstream television channels for the audience's attention

 Discuss which, if any, serial narratives hold the loyalty of class members | Assess:
 • understanding of the influence of social and cultural contexts on representations in *Cuffs*
 • understanding of the influence of social and cultural contexts on the popularity of crime drama for audiences and producers

 Homework:
 Watch one other crime drama and compare the social issues it explores with those in *Cuffs*. |

Week	Component(s) Media form(s) Set product(s)	Aims/Area of framework	Learning objectives Learners will be able to:	Activities	Assessment/Homework
7	C1 Television *Cuffs*	To explore television **media industries,** especially regulation, and how *Cuffs* fits the BBC	• State the requirements of public service broadcasting • Explain the role of Ofcom in regulating television • Explain the special requirement for the BBC to be distinctive as a publicly funded institution • State what is meant by 'Reithian values' and how these have helped establish the BBC as a global brand • Discuss in what ways and how far *Cuffs* meets PSB requirements • State how the BBC uses its digital platform to create convergence	Exposition: Ofcom and PSB Discuss what the class know about the BBC, the licence fee and what it stands for Exposition: the BBC charter, 'Reithian values' and BBC Worldwide List the ways *Cuffs* does and doesn't fit PSB requirements Discuss the use of BBC Three by class members – why might its audience have declined since moving to online only?	Assess: • understanding of role of Ofcom in regulating PSB television (and radio) • identification of the BBC's role to educate, inform and entertain • understanding of the ways in which *Cuffs* fits PSB and the competing demands of audience success • ability to exemplify convergence by citing the BBC iPlayer **Homework:** Produce a PowerPoint presentation showing how the BBC is responding to audience tastes through the programme mix and available platforms.
8	C1 Television *The Avengers*	Screen *The Avengers* episode Analyse **representation** in *The Avengers*	• Analyse the social groups present in and absent from *The Avengers* • Discuss the reasons for this presence/absence	Create a character list for *The Avengers* episode and review for inclusion/ exclusion – noting deliberate attempts at inclusion by the producers	Assess: • ability to explain selection in representation • ability to explain stereotyping

No.	Topic				
			• Discuss the use of stereotypes (and/or anti-stereotypes) in *The Avengers* – especially gender stereotypes • Analyse the messages and values in *The Avengers*	Analyse key sequences for representation Outline the narrative of *The Avengers* episode and discuss the messages and values communicated by this narrative	• understanding of the underlying messages and values, e.g. what is being celebrated or criticised in the programme, and how these are shared by other media products **Homework:** Watch at least one other episode of *The Avengers*.
9	C1 Television *The Avengers* *Cuffs*	To analyse key differences in **representations** between *The Avengers* and *Cuffs* To analyse how these reflect historical social and cultural **contexts** To sample other mid-60s TV products	• Explain how the gender representations reflect the historical and contemporary social and cultural contexts of the two products • Explain how the representations of sexualities reflect the historical and contemporary social and cultural contexts of the two products • Explain how the representations of race and ethnicity reflect the historical and contemporary social and cultural contexts of the two products	Exposition: changing gender roles in the 1960s (pre-1970s feminism but post-'sexual revolution') Discuss the gender differences in the roles of Steed and Emma in *The Avengers* episode and compare to gender roles in *Cuffs* Exposition: illegality of male gay sex in the early 1960s Discuss the assumption of heterosexuality in *The Avengers* episode and compare to the leading gay character in *Cuffs* Exposition: assumption of a common 'white' culture in 1960s Britain, despite presence of minorities Compare the white representation in *The Avengers* to the multiculturalism of *Cuffs*	**Homework:** Essay: 'How do television programmes reflect different historical contexts? Use *The Avengers* and *Cuffs* to illustrate your answer.'

Week	Component(s) Media form(s) Set product(s)	Aims/Area of framework	Learning objectives Learners will be able to:	Activities	Assessment/Homework
			 ● Explain how representations of threats to social order reflect the historical and contemporary social and cultural contexts of the two products ● Consider the effect of different audience expectations in how 1960s and 2010s audiences might interpret the different representations	Exposition: fear of Russian spies in Cold War 1960s Britain Discuss how the threat of replacement 'insiders' in *The Avengers* reflects the paranoia generated by the Cold War, compared with the more everyday threat of crime in *Cuffs* Discuss what the episode of *The Avengers* suggests about audience expectations of representations and how this audience might interpret *Cuffs*	
10	C1 Television The Avengers	To analyse **media language** in *The Avengers* – analysing key sequences in terms of ML elements	● Analyse the camerawork in sequences from *The Avengers* ● Analyse the soundtrack in sequences from *The Avengers* ● Analyse the mise-en-scène in sequences from *The Avengers* ● Analyse the editing in sequences from *The Avengers* ● State any use of intertextuality in the sequences	In-depth analysis of short sequences from *The Avengers*	Assess: ● ability to accurately use technical terms ● ability to analyse media language elements and their connotations

			Learning activities	Exposition / discussion	Homework / Assessment
					Homework: Watch the opening sequence of a second episode of *The Avengers*. Analyse the use of media language in creating meaning for an audience. Identify at least one use of each of the four technical areas of camerawork, editing, mise-en-scène and sound. Write up the analysis in approximately 200 words.
11	C1 Television *The Avengers* *Cuffs*	To analyse *The Avengers* episode in terms of 'macro' **media language** (genre and narrative) To apply narrative theory to *The Avengers* and *Cuffs*	● State the generic conventions of the spy drama and exemplify using *The Avengers* ● Explain how the episode of *The Avengers* creates the narrative resolution required for a series narrative ● Compare this narrative with that in the *Cuffs* serial narrative ● State Propp's character categories: villain, hero, princess, donor, helper, dispatcher, false hero ● Exemplify Propp's characters from *The Avengers* and *Cuffs*	Exposition/discussion: What are the key conventions of a spy drama (e.g. secret state or quasi-state organisations, narrative revolves around combating plots, use of spy technology, suspense and peril)? Review of serial/series distinction: compare the closed narrative of *The Avengers* with the open narrative of *Cuffs* Exposition – Propp's character categories – application to a mythic film narrative the students all know (e.g. *The Lion King*, *Star Wars*) Discussion: How well does this theory work for the two television programmes?	**Assess:** ● knowledge of spy drama conventions and ability to exemplify ● understanding of series and serial narrative structures ● knowledge and understanding of Propp's theory **Homework:** Essay: 'How far do *Cuffs* and *The Avengers* tell similar stories to be popular with mass audiences?'

Scheme of Work

Week	Component(s) Media form(s) Set product(s)	Aims/Area of framework	Learning objectives Learners will be able to:	Activities	Assessment/Homework
12	C1 Television *The Avengers* *Cuffs*	To compare and contrast *The Avengers* and *Cuffs* in terms of **audience** To explore **media industries** and *The Avengers*	● Outline and compare the uses and gratifications offered by *Cuffs* and *The Avengers* ● Explain how ITV targets both a prime-time adult British audience and international sales ● State the dominance of ITV as the only commercial channel in the three-channel 1960s	Review uses and gratifications theory and discuss how it can be applied to different media forms and to different genres of TV programme Discuss the uses and gratifications offered by *The Avengers* and *Cuffs* Discuss the prominence of PSB broadcasting (news, current affairs, classical music, single plays) on the ITV schedules – November 1965 *TVTimes* available at: https://radiosoundsfamiliar.com/the-tv-times-archive-1960s.php Discuss how *The Avengers* fits a prime-time post-watershed mass audience Research how the fourth series was changed to help international sales – see: http://theavengers.tv/forever/peel1-prod.htm	Assess: ● knowledge and understanding of the target audiences (national and international) for *The Avengers* ● knowledge of three-channel television of the 1960s **Homework:** Short essay: 'Explore the uses and gratifications of television dramas. Use one programme you have studied to illustrate your answer.'

| 13 | C2 Radio | To explore radio in terms of **media industries, audience** and **contexts** | • Identify the regulator for radio
• Identify different types of radio station: international (e.g. the World Service), national and local broadcast, online, commercial and public service broadcasting
• Identify the target audience for BBC Radios 1 to 6 in terms of their content
• State which BBC radio channels best meet PSB requirements
• State the outlines of the political debate as to whether or not Radio 1 should be privatised | Research online commercial stations, broadcast commercial radio on Wikipedia, and PSB BBC stations on iPlayer

Research target audiences and content for BBC stations in the BBC annual report 2016/17, page 27, and discuss how the descriptions of each channel emphasise their PSB elements

Discuss how effectively the BBC reaches all audiences with its radio stations

Exposition: the cultural context in which different genres of music are valued or seen as trivial, and live performance is seen as more valuable than recorded music

Discuss the political context in which Radio 3 has a small audience yet a large budget but its existence is never questioned by politicians, while Radio 1 is attacked as 'too commercial' | Assess:
• ability to identify Ofcom as the radio regulator
• understanding of the contexts in which Radio 1 operates – social/cultural and political
• understanding of the role of Radio 1 within BBC radio

Homework:

Take notes following set questions on Ofcom.

Listen to three BBC radio stations not previously accessed and note the differences in style and content.

Write a short proposal for a new digital BBC radio station targeted at 6–12 year olds, emphasising the PSB elements. |

Week	Component(s) Media form(s) Set product(s)	Aims/Area of framework	Learning objectives Learners will be able to:	Activities	Assessment/Homework
14	C2 Radio *Radio 1 Live Lounge*	To analyse **audience** address in terms of its content and style	• State the target audience for Radio 1 • Suggest the uses and gratifications offered by BBC Radio 1 *Live Lounge* • Suggest how audiences might interpret BBC Radio 1 *Live Lounge* differently depending on fandom • Identify and discuss how Radio 1 *Live Lounge* uses BBC iPlayer to reach audiences • Explain how Radio 1 *Live Lounge* tries to fit the BBC's PSB requirements	Review uses and gratifications theory and discuss how it can be applied to different BBC radio stations View BBC Live Lounge content and discuss the uses and gratifications offered Explore differences within the class in reaction to and interpretation of the content; discuss the role of gender, age, fandom or any other factor in different interpretations Discuss how far the choice of presenter, the choice of music played and the emphasis on live performance fulfil the BBC's PSB requirement to be distinctive, to reflect diversity within the UK, to create innovative and challenging content, and to serve all audiences	**Homework:** Write up the media audience analysis of Radio 1 *Live Lounge* from the lesson. Essay: 'How does BBC music radio fulfil the BBC's PSB requirements to be distinctive, to reflect diversity within the UK, to create innovative and challenging content, and to serve all audiences? Refer to the *Live Lounge* in your answer.'

| 15 | C2
Music videos
Chosen products | Analyse the **media language** and **representations** in the chosen set music videos in terms of social/cultural **contexts**

To explore possible differences in **audience** interpretations

To explore how audiences use fandom and music videos to construct their identity | • Explain the influence of patriarchy and feminism (or post-feminism) on representations in the chosen set music videos

• Explain the influence of multiculturalism on representations in the chosen set music videos

• Explain the influence of changing attitudes to sexualities on representations in the chosen set music videos

• Explain the influence of the dominance of celebrity culture on the chosen set music videos

• Suggest how audiences might interpret music videos differently depending on gender, age and fandom

• Explain how fans of music artists may use their fandom to help construct an identity (e.g. through a sense of belonging) | Review the previous media language and representation analyses of the set music videos

Discuss the representation of gender, race/ethnicity and sexualities in the set videos in relation to social contexts

Discuss how far each video is influenced by celebrity culture (e.g. in the emphasis on the performer and performance rather than the song)

Discuss the role of the music video in promoting celebrity culture

Explore differences within the class in reaction to, and interpretation of, the videos; discuss the role of gender, age, fandom or any other factor in different reactions or interpretations

Explore how far students identify with artists or feel they belong to a fan group and why this may be particularly significant for young people exploring their place in the world | **Homework:**
Essay: 'How do fans of music artists use their fandom to help construct an identity? Provide examples.'

Write up the celebrity culture notes from lesson and then write an essay.

Essay: 'Analyse the representations in one music video you have studied, including in relation to its social and cultural contexts.' |

Week	Component(s) Media form(s) Set product(s)	Aims/Area of framework	Learning objectives Learners will be able to:	Activities	Assessment/Homework
16	C2 Music magazines *MOJO*	To explore the influence of social/cultural **contexts** on music magazines To analyse the influence of social/cultural **contexts** on **representations** in *MOJO* magazine	● Explain the influence of popular music from previous decades on media representations, particularly those aimed at older audiences ● Explain the influence of gender roles in popular music on media representations ● Explain the influence of racial and ethnic affiliations on representations of different types of popular music ● Analyse the influence of contexts on *MOJO* front covers	Review the previous media language and representation analyses of *MOJO* magazine Discuss the influence of contexts such as the high esteem afforded 'classic rock' by the baby-boomer generation, the largely sexist roles offered to women within that musical genre, the dominance of white British and American musicians in that genre In-depth analysis of the influence of contexts on two *MOJO* front covers Comparison study of one other front cover from a different genre of music	**Homework:** Write up notes from the lesson on the influence of gender roles in popular music on media representations. Essay: 'How do the music magazines you have studied use media representations in the same way and differently?' Essay: 'Analyse the representations in one music magazine you have studied, including in relation to its social and cultural contexts.'
17	C2 Music magazines *MOJO*	To investigate media **industries** and **audience** for *MOJO* magazine	● Explain how the Bauer group is diversified over media forms and products ● Identify the funding for *MOJO* magazine ● Identify that the newspaper and magazine industries can choose to be self-regulated	Research the Bauer group range of brands and their audience reach (in terms of age and gender categories) on the Bauer website http://www.bauermedia.co.uk/	Assess: ● ability to identify IPSO as the self-regulator for *MOJO* ● understanding of the media industrial background of *MOJO* magazine

No.	Topic	Learning objectives	Activities	Assessment / Homework
		• Explain how *MOJO* uses convergence through its website • Outline how different Bauer products target different audiences • Suggest the uses and gratifications offered by *MOJO* • Explain different possible audience interpretations of *MOJO*	Exposition: magazine funding – circulation, advertising, events, etc.; lack of regulation of print media due to ideals of 'press freedom' means that *MOJO* has joined IPSO as the regulator run by the newspaper and magazine industry Exploration of *MOJO* website Discussion of the uses and gratifications offered generally by magazines and specifically by *MOJO* Explore differences within the class in reaction to, and interpretation of, the magazine; discuss the role of gender, age, fandom or any other factor in different reactions or interpretations	• understanding of media audiences for magazines, including *MOJO* **Homework:** Write up media industries notes on IPSO for *MOJO* from the lesson. Essay: 'How are the music magazines you have studied regulated and identify their target audience.'
18	C2 Newspapers	To explore **media language** and genre conventions on newspapers – the 'quality' and 'tabloid' press To explore political **contexts** for newspapers • State the generic conventions of 'quality' and 'tabloid' newspapers • Discuss the political influence of print newspapers and their political leanings • Outline political debates about the regulation of print newspapers	Analyse at least two examples each of tabloid and quality Sunday newspaper front pages (e.g. *The Sun*, *The Mirror*, *The Observer*, *The Daily Telegraph*) to ascertain generic conventions in terms of layout, typography, use of images and language, and content	Assess: • identification of generic conventions • ability to analyse front pages and suggest connotations • understanding of the political contexts in which newspapers operate

Scheme of Work

Week	Component(s) Media form(s) Set product(s)	Aims/Area of framework	Learning objectives Learners will be able to:	Activities	Assessment/Homework
				Compare *The Observer* and *The Mirror* with *The Sun* and *The Telegraph* on one political issue to elicit different political leanings	**Homework:** Research press freedom around the world using https://rsf.org/en/ranking#
				Exposition: how the political role of newspapers in criticising or supporting political parties and commenting on policies depends on their freedom from the PSB requirement to be impartial, hence the demand for a free press not to be regulated or controlled by the state	
				Research the Leveson Inquiry and the subsequent debates about press regulation	
19	C2 Newspapers Online *The Observer*	To investigate **media industry** issues for newspapers, including *The Observer*	● Identify the sources of funding for newspapers ● Identify IPSO and IMPRESS as two competing self-regulators ● Explain the difficulties faced by newspapers due to declining circulation and advertising revenue following competition from the internet	Exposition: funding sources – circulation, print advertising, online advertising, sponsored content, online paywalls, events, membership, etc.; IPSO and IMPRESS and Leveson compliance; decline in advertising revenue and circulation for print newspapers	Assess: ● ability to identify sources of funding for newspapers ● ability to identify IPSO and IMPRESS as regulators ● ability to discuss why online-only newspapers are not regulated

			Learning outcomes	Activities	Homework
19			• State an example of online newspapers' paywalls • State the global reach of online versions of newspapers • Identify online-only newspapers such as BuzzFeed • Explain why online-only newspapers are not regulated	Research: online *Guardian/Observer* and *Mail* international reach; BuzzFeed as an example of an online-only newspaper Discuss: the difficulties of regulating an international online newspaper	**Homework:** Research and note any differences between British newspapers and an online version of an American newspaper, e.g. *The New York Times*.
20	C2 Newspapers *The Observer*	To investigate *The Observer's* target **audience** and media **industry's** values and beliefs	• Outline the effects of the ownership of the GMG by the Scott Trust • State *The Observer's* target audience: progressive, educated, middle class, mixed gender • Explain *The Guardian/Observer's* social and political ethos • Identify that *The Guardian/Observer* have chosen not to place online content behind a paywall but ask for voluntary membership to fund the newspaper in an era of declining sales • Discuss the uses and gratifications offered by such a membership model	Exposition: the Scott Trust and editorial independence; *The Guardian/Observer* print and online audiences Analyse headlines of comment pieces and editorials in *The Observer* to exemplify the ethos of the organisation Access *Guardian/Observer* online to note repeated exhortations to join the membership scheme (but note that Plan B is to create a paywall) Apply uses and gratifications theory to this membership model	**Homework:** Essay: 'How do newspapers reflect the media industries that own them? Use *The Observer* as an example.'

Week	Component(s) Media form(s) Set product(s)	Aims/Area of framework	Learning objectives Learners will be able to:	Activities	Assessment/Homework
21	C2 Newspapers *The Observer*	To analyse **representations** and **media language** in *The Observer* print edition	● Analyse two *Observer* front covers in terms of layout, typography, language use, images, graphics and colour ● Identify key elements of *The Observer* house style ● State how *The Observer* uses the advantages of print technology on its front page ● Identify any use of intertextuality on the front pages ● Analyse representations in two front covers of *The Observer*	In-depth analysis of two front covers Comparison of the media language of the front covers with an inside news and opinion page in the main section of *The Observer* to identify the house style Discussion of the advantages of print technology – the ability to produce lengthy and detailed copy, the ability to use layout for impact (e.g. headlines, large images), etc. Discuss the view of the world constructed by the *Observer* pages studied	**Homework:** Pick one other quality newspaper and note how it differs in media language from *The Observer*.
22	C2 Newspapers *The Observer*	To analyse differences in **representations** and **media language** in historical *Observer* front pages	● Analyse how the media language style in the three historical *Observer* front covers differs from the contemporary editions ● Analyse differences in representations in news stories in the three historical *Observer* front covers from the contemporary editions	Analyse the key difference in media language between contemporary and historical editions, e.g. monochrome versus colour, fewer stories on the front page and greater use of images in the contemporary editions, less formal language use in the contemporary editions (e.g. in how politicians	Assess: ● understanding of key differences in representation and media language

			are named), greater use of marketing on the front pages in the contemporary editions, more cluttered, 'newsy' layout in the historical editions Analyse key differences in representation, e.g. greater prominence of female leaders, different sexualities and racial/ethnic minorities in the contemporary editions, the mention of equal pay for women as not yet attainable and the article suggesting that a 'mixed-race' marriage was news in the historical editions, the emphasis on strikes and industrial relations Analyse continuities in representation – concerns over Europe and Russia	**Homework:** Look online at images of other 1960s newspapers. Discuss with people in their 60s and older what life was like in the 1960s.
23	C2 Newspapers *The Observer*	To compare contemporary and historical editions of the print newspaper in terms of how these reflect historical changes in social, cultural and political **contexts**	● Describe and exemplify the continuities in how media contexts influence media language and representations in the contemporary and historical editions of *The Observer*	Discussion: What do the historical front covers suggest about life in mid-1960s Britain (e.g. that it was dominated by white heterosexual males, very few women were in positions of power, 'race' was about people who were 'different', Britain was worried about the threat from Russia, from strikes, and whether it should join 'Europe')?	**Homework:** Essay: 'How do newspapers reflect the historical, social and cultural contexts in which they are produced? Refer to *The Observer* in your answer.'

Scheme of Work

Week	Component(s) Media form(s) Set product(s)	Aims/Area of framework	Learning objectives Learners will be able to:	Activities	Assessment/Homework
			● Describe and exemplify the changes in how media contexts influence representations in the contemporary and historical editions of *The Observer*	How is this similar to the Britain represented in *The Avengers*? In what ways does this differ from contemporary Britain? (e.g. the influence of feminism, multiculturalism, equality for sexualities, Britain is worried about the threat from Russia and how or whether it should leave 'Europe', while trades unions have declined in power and strikes are rarer)	
24	Online *The Observer*	To analyse the **media language** and **representations** in terms of the **audience** address and the ethos of the online *Observer*	● Analyse the homepage and at least one other page in terms of layout, typography, images, graphics, language use, colour, links and embedded audio-visual material ● Discuss how the *Observer* house style reflects the ethos of the newspaper ● Discuss how *The Observer* house style reflects the generic conventions of a 'quality' newspaper ● Analyse the representations on the *Observer* homepage	In-depth analysis of the website	**Homework:** Essay: 'To what extent is the online *Observer* a continuation of the print version?'

25	Online *The Observer*	To compare the **media language** and **representations** in *The Guardian/Observer* Twitter and Instagram feeds with the newspaper website To analyse and exemplify **audience** participation in the social media feeds and 'Comment is free' pages	● Analyse *The Guardian/Observer* Twitter feed and Instagram feed in terms of layout, typography, images, graphics, language use, colour, links and embedded audio-visual material ● Compare these with the house style of the website ● Compare representations in *The Guardian/Observer* Twitter feed and Instagram feed with those on the website ● Discuss opportunities for the audience to participate in discussions in social media and the 'Comment is free' pages of *The Guardian* website ● Cite examples of different audience interpretations of articles	● Discuss how these representations address *The Observer* target audience and reflect *The Observer*'s values and beliefs, especially in relation to inclusivity and avoiding stereotyping ● Identify the influence of media contexts on the online newspaper In-depth analysis of Twitter and Instagram feeds Discussion: to what extent the audience is truly active on these feeds or simply reacting to the agenda set by the newspaper Select two examples of comments on articles in the 'Comment is free' pages that adopt a radically different position from that taken by the original article	Assess: ● ability to accurately use technical terms ● ability to analyse media language elements and their connotations ● ability to analyse representations ● ability to cite at least one similarity and at least one difference between the feeds and the website ● understanding of audience activity/passivity **Homework:** Make notes on the differences between the Twitter and Instagram feeds of a celebrity and those of the newspaper.

45

Week	Component(s) Media form(s) Set product(s)	Aims/Area of framework	Learning objectives Learners will be able to:	Activities	Assessment/Homework
26		Mock exams			
27		Mock exams			
28		Revision and exam practice, including: • denotation and connotation • uses and gratifications • textual analysis comparison of *MOJO* magazine and one other unseen music magazine	• Recall media language terminology from previous sessions • Practise denotation and connotation examples using media language • Analyse the ways in which media producers use media language to create meanings for audiences • Analyse *MOJO* magazine and *UNCUT* magazine front covers in terms of media language (e.g. layout, typography, image, graphics, colour and language use) • Repeat and practise media language terminology	Check recall and understanding of media language. In pairs using computers, research the uses and gratifications theory and discuss how it can be applied to different magazines Share notes on denotation/ connotation and the uses and gratifications theory from previous lesson for recap Whole-class discussion on denotation/connotation and the uses and gratifications theory Feed back paired analysis of magazine media language comparison Complete the timed writing activity: 'How far is media language used differently on *MOJO* magazine and *UNCUT* magazine front covers to reflect genre conventions?'	**Homework:** Write up notes on denotation/connotation and the uses and gratifications theory from the lesson and research further music magazine examples. Revise denotation/ connotation, the uses and gratifications theory, and media language of *MOJO* magazine and other music magazines.

			Homework
29	Revision and exam practice, including: • textual analysis of *Cuffs* and *The Avengers* extracts • perspectives on representation • genre and narrative theory	• Make notes under timed conditions • Identify key media terminology from key sequences • Compare and contrast representations found in *Cuffs* and *The Avengers* • Compare and contrast narrative and genre in the crime and spy genres	Practise and evaluate different techniques for making notes on unseen television extracts Produce revision guides on representation, genre, narrative and audience appeal for the two television products	**Homework:** Revise media contexts for both television products.
30	Revision and exam practice, including: • media industries terminology • textual analysis of *The Lego Movie* advertising	• Recall media industries terms and definitions • Analyse the ways in which regulation supports media industries • Understand the benefits of synergy within the film industry • Analyse and apply genre codes • Recall Blumler and Katz's uses and gratifications theory in relation to video games	Industries test Regulatory logo recognition game Discuss role of regulation in film and video games Practice question on synergy and discussion of benefits Reviews of representation, media language, especially intertextuality and generic codes and conventions in the trailer and posters Recall uses and gratifications theory	**Homework:** Produce a revision sheet focusing on industry regulatory bodies and their role. Write a timed model answer to the following question: 'How does *The Lego Movie* video game provide uses and gratifications to its audience? Refer to Blumler and Katz's theory in your answer.'

Week	Component(s) Media form(s) Set product(s)	Aims/Area of framework	Learning objectives Learners will be able to:	Activities	Assessment/Homework
31		Revision and exam practice, including: • active and passive audiences • textual analysis of *The Observer* in print and online	• Apply the concepts of active and passive audiences across a range of media forms • Explain key elements of media industries for newspapers • Analyse unseen print and online newspapers in terms of media language and representation	List different forms of audience activity for TV, advertising, video games, music videos, radio and online media forms Ranking forms for the degree of activity/passivity Media industries quiz Practise media language and representation exam questions	**Homework:** Revise for the whole exam.
32		Revision and exam practice, including media contexts: • Comparison of Cuffs and The Avengers in relation to contexts • Comparison of contemporary and historical editions of The Observer in relation to contexts	• Compare *Cuffs* and *The Avengers* in relation to contexts • Compare contemporary and historical editions of *The Observer* in relation to contexts	Revise products and contexts and set individual practice exam essays	**Homework:** Revise for the whole exam.

Year 1 Week 1a

Introduction to the course – media forms

Learning objectives – learners will be able to:

- identify the nine media forms
- reflect on their own consumption/use of media products
- understand the structure of the GCSE course.

Teacher activities

- Ask learners to list all the media forms they can think of and write down how many hours they spend consuming/using these forms each week, then to compare their lists with another member of the class.
- Explain that, in GCSE Media Studies, the nine forms that must be studied are: television; film; radio; newspapers; magazines; advertising and marketing; online, social and participatory media; video games; music video.
- Using the official GCSE Media Studies forms listed above, ask learners to number the forms according to how important and influential they think they are. They must be prepared to explain why.
- Manage feedback and discussion on the contemporary significance and influence of the media forms.

Learner activities

- Learners explore their own knowledge of the nine media forms and reflect on their roles as consumers/users of media products.
- In pairs and as a class, learners discuss the significance of the nine media forms in their lives as consumers/users of media products.
- Learners think up an acronym for the nine forms.
- Learners make notes on the structure of the GCSE Media Studies course.
- Learners make a note of media terminology, with definitions.

Suggested homework

Learners name three products they particularly enjoy in three different media forms and explain why.

Year 1 Week 1b

Introduction to the course – theoretical framework

Learning objectives – learners will be able to:

- identify the nine media forms
- state the four areas of the theoretical framework
- apply one of the four areas of the theoretical framework to a media product.

Key product

Fantastic Beasts and Where to Find Them (2016) IMAX and theatrical posters (https://christhilk. com/2016/11/16/movie-marketing-madness-fantastic-beasts-and-where-to-find-them/)

Teacher activities

- Direct a quick test/recap of the nine media forms.
- Explain that learners will analyse media products by using the following four areas of the theoretical framework, giving brief explanations of each area:
  - **Media language** – How do the media use forms, codes and conventions to communicate meanings to their audiences?
  - **Representation** – How are people, places, events and issues portrayed in the media?
  - **Media industries** – How are media products funded and how are they affected by the industries that produce them?
  - **Audiences** – How are audiences targeted and how do they respond to media products?
- Display the poster for *Fantastic Beasts and Where to Find Them*, then split the class into four groups, assigning one of the four areas to each group. Ask each group to write down three points about the poster related to their area of the framework.
- Manage feedback, guiding learners to apply the four areas of the theoretical framework.

Learner activities

- Learners recall the nine media forms.
- Learners note down the four areas of the theoretical framework.
- In groups, learners apply one area of the theoretical framework to the IMAX and/or theatrical posters for *Fantastic Beasts and Where to Find Them.*
- Learners feed back their analysis to the whole class.

Suggested homework

Learners select one film poster and annotate it, using one area of the theoretical framework.

Year 1 Week 2a

Introduction to media language – print

Learning objectives – learners will be able to:

- analyse examples of layout, typography, language use, use of images, graphics and colour
- suggest connotations for examples of media language use
- analyse the ways in which media producers use media language to create meanings for audiences.

Key products

1953 *Hoover* **advertisement** – 'Christmas morning she'll be happier with a Hoover' (http://neatdesigns.net/35-extremely-sexist-ads-that-you-should-see/)

1961 *Kenwood Chef* **advertisement** – 'The Chef does everything but cook – that's what wives are for!' (https://skell091.wordpress.com/2013/03/21/media-discourse-analysis-semiotic-print-advertisement-analysis/)

2015 Sport England's *This Girl Can* – 'I'm slow but I'm lapping everyone on the couch' (https://www.theguardian.com/media-network/2015/may/26/eight-ads-shatter-gender-stereotypes)

Teacher activities

- Give learners a list of key terms and their definitions for print analysis, including: layout, typography, colour, language, denotation, connotation, messages, values. (See the glossary at the end of these resources.)
- Display the 1953 *Hoover* advertisement for whole-class analysis, giving learners a brief historical/sociological background.
- Direct whole-class analysis and discussion of the *Hoover* advertisement, encouraging learners to try out and apply the key terms.

Learner activities

- As a class, learners discuss and analyse the *Hoover* advertisement, learning to apply the correct terminology.
- In pairs, learners analyse and compare (making written notes) the *Kenwood Chef* and the *This Girl Can* advertisements, identifying denotations, connotations, messages and values. It may be helpful to give learners a table or a list of questions to aid their analysis.
- Learners feed back their findings to the whole class.

Suggested homework

Learners write up their analysis of one of the three key products.

Year 1 Week 2b

Introduction to media language – print and online

> ### Learning objectives – learners will be able to:
>
> - analyse examples of layout, typography, language use, use of images, graphics and colour
> - suggest connotations for examples of media language use
> - analyse the ways in which media producers use contrasting media language to address their audiences.

Key products

Kerrang! magazine, 14 January 2017 (https://pbs.twimg.com/media/C103eEsWEAAMiPX.jpg)

BBC Music Magazine, June 2015 (http://www.classical-music.com/issue/june-2015)

Teacher activities

- Recap (perhaps using a brief test) the key terms for print analysis, checking learners' understanding of denotation and connotation. Reinforce the terms 'genre' and 'generic conventions'. Explain that producers target different audiences through their use of media language.
- Display the front covers of *Kerrang!* and *BBC Music Magazine* side by side. Ask learners to write down which audiences are being targeted through the use of contrasting media language in the two music magazines and to give reasons for their answers, using the correct terms.
- Give learners a list of key terms and their definitions for online analysis (see the glossary at the end of these resources).
- Using computers, ask learners to make notes on the contrasting media language used in the websites for *Kerrang!* and *BBC Music Magazine* (http://www.kerrang.com/; http://www.classical-music.com/).

Learner activities

- Learners check recall and understanding of print analysis terms.
- Learners analyse and compare (making written notes) the ways in which *Kerrang!* and *BBC Music Magazine* target different audiences through using contrasting media language.
- Learners research and analyse the contrasting media language used in *Kerrang!*'s and *BBC Music Magazine*'s online counterparts.

Suggested homework

Learners write up a comparison of the homepages of *Kerrang!* and *BBC Music Magazine*.

Year 1 Week 3a

Introduction to media language – audio-visual

Learning objectives – learners will be able to:

- analyse examples of camerawork, editing, mise-en-scène and soundtrack
- suggest connotations for examples of media language use
- recognise generic conventions of crime drama.

Key product

'Schooled in Murder', *Midsomer Murders*, Series 15, Episode 6, ITV (available on DVD)

Teacher activities

- Screen the opening sequence and titles of 'Schooled in Murder'. Ask learners to identify key elements which fit the genre of crime drama.
- Give learners a list of key terms and their definitions for moving image analysis, including: camerawork, editing, mise-en-scène and soundtrack (see the glossary).
- Divide learners into four groups, allocating one of the key media language elements to each group for analysis. Screen the extract twice more, allowing learners time to make notes and to discuss their views.
- Direct group feedback and discussion of the extract, encouraging learners to try out and apply the key terms. If time allows, encourage a discussion of connotations, messages and values.

Learner activities

- In pairs, learners identify, note down and feed back key elements from the sequence which fit the genre of crime drama.
- In groups, learners analyse and feed back to the class their points on the effects of the four key elements of media language.

Suggested homework

Learners write up an analysis of one of the key elements of media language in the extract.

Year 1 Week 3b

Introduction to media language – audio-visual

Learning objectives – learners will be able to:
● analyse examples of camerawork, editing, mise-en-scène and soundtrack
● suggest connotations for examples of media language use
● recognise generic conventions of crime drama.

Key product

'Game', *Endeavour*, Series 4, Episode 1, ITV (available on DVD)

Teacher activities

● Screen the first five minutes of 'Game' (including the opening sequence and titles).

● Ask learners to identify key elements which fit the genre of crime drama. How similar to/different from those in the *Midsomer Murders* extract are they?

● Screen the extract a second time, asking learners to pick two of the key media language elements to analyse.

● Ask learners to storyboard the title sequence of a new crime drama aimed at a youth audience.

Learner activities

● Learners identify, note down and feed back key elements from the sequence which fit the genre of crime drama, considering similarities to and differences from *Midsomer Murders*.

● Learners select two of the four key media language elements to analyse and make notes on these during the second screening of *Endeavour*.

● In pairs, learners storyboard the title sequence of a new crime drama aimed at a youth audience.

Suggested homework

Learners log different types of media language use in a TV sitcom and in a reality TV programme of their choice.

Year 1 Week 4a

Introduction to media representations – music videos

> ## Learning objectives – learners will be able to:
>
> - state how media producers have chosen to select representational elements and not select others
> - analyse gender stereotypes in music videos.

Key products

Paramore, *The Only Exception* (https://www.youtube.com/watch?v=-J7J_IWUhls)
P!nk, *Stupid Girls* (https://www.youtube.com/watch?v=BR4yQFZK9YM)

Teacher activities

- Give learners two definitions of stereotyping.
- Ask learners to list common stereotypes associated with masculinity and femininity.
- Manage a discussion on common stereotypes, using learners' feedback.
- Screen *The Only Exception* by Paramore, asking learners to consider the stereotypical representations of gender and the ways in which those stereotypes are constructed through media language.
- Screen *Stupid Girls* by P!nk. How do the representations of gender differ in this music video?

Learner activities

- In groups, learners list and feed back to the class common stereotypes associated with masculinity and femininity, noting disagreements.
- Learners write notes on how far these common stereotypes are reflected in *The Only Exception* by Paramore, considering how media language is used to construct those stereotypes.
- Learners write notes on how far these common stereotypes are challenged in *Stupid Girls* by P!nk, considering media language.
- As a class, learners discuss why music video producers have selected certain representational elements and not others.

Suggested homework

Learners produce a mock-up for a CD front cover for a new artist with an anti-stereotypical representation of gender.

Year 1 Week 4b

Introduction to media representations – music videos, advertising and marketing

---

Learning objectives – learners will be able to:

- state how media producers have chosen to select representational elements and not select others
- analyse gender stereotypes in music videos and advertising
- suggest how the construction of reality in music videos and advertising might fit the producers' purposes.

Key products

One Direction, *Live While We're Young* (www.youtube.com/watch?v=AbPED9bisSc)

Pepsi's *Live for Now* advertisement with One Direction (www.youtube.com/watch?v=Sfy8UYRhmpA)

Teacher activities

- Ask learners to suggest reasons for the success of One Direction from 2010–12 and to write down six adjectives to describe the brand image of the band.
- Screen *Live While We're Young* (2012) by One Direction, asking learners to identify how the band, their fans and 'reality' are represented.
- Screen Pepsi's *Live for Now* advertisement with One Direction, from 2012. Ask learners to discuss this statement from Mark Hardy, Syco/Sony Marketing Director: 'The essence of the strategy was not to position One Direction as demi-gods but as "my mate" the girls could have access to 24/7. Behind the scenes we did extensive social media training with the boys so they understood how to respond to a tweet' (www.campaignlive.co.uk/article/lessons-marketers-learn-one-direction-brand-phenomenon/1208304#JOKHVQAS4fWqGU20.99).

Learner activities

- Learners analyse the representations of One Direction, their fans and 'reality' in *Live While We're Young* and in Pepsi's *Live for Now* advertisement, considering how far these fit or challenge stereotypes.
- Learners explore the marketing strategy used to promote One Direction, considering how far the band members were represented as 'my mate' as opposed to 'demi-gods'.

Suggested homework

Learners collect two examples of anti-stereotyping in advertisements and two examples of anti-stereotyping in music videos.

Year 1 Week 5a

Introduction to media audiences

Learning objectives – learners will be able to:

- state examples of television and radio channels with mass and niche audiences
- discuss how audiences may be passive and/or active in a range of media forms: television, music videos, magazines, video games and online/participatory media.

Key products

TV and radio listings magazines, such as: *Radio Times, TVTimes*

Teacher activities

- Explain the terms mass, niche and target audiences.
- Ask learners to identify target audiences from front covers of *Radio Times* and *TVTimes* and from TV and radio schedules.
- Give a brief outline of debates over active and passive audiences (http://www.bbc.co.uk/education/guides/zg24frd/revision/3).
- Explain the uses and gratifications theory (Blumler and Katz).

Learner activities

- In pairs, learners compare the front covers of *Radio Times* and *TVTimes*, identifying the different target audiences.
- Learners look at two sets of schedules for different channels for the same day: one from BBC 1 and one from BBC 4. How far are these channels aimed at mass or niche audiences? Consider age, gender and class.
- Learners write down one example that they enjoy of each of the following: a television programme; a video game; a magazine; a music video; an app. Using Blumler and Katz's theory of uses and gratifications, they write down the top two ways in which they actively use each programme.
- Learners discuss which of these media forms they use in the most active way and which they use most passively.

Suggested homework

Learners log their own media use over one day and evaluate its activity/passivity.

Year 1 Week 5b

Introduction to media audiences

> ### Learning objectives – learners will be able to:
>
> - state examples of television and radio channels with mass and niche audiences
> - discuss how audiences may be passive and/or active in a range of media forms: television, radio and online/participatory media.

Key products

BBC 1 homepage – http://www.bbc.co.uk/bbcone

E4 homepage – http://www.channel4.com/programmes/e4-homepage

Radio 2 homepage – http://www.bbc.co.uk/radio2

Radio 1 homepage – http://www.bbc.co.uk/radio1

Teacher activities

- Ask learners to analyse and compare the homepages of BBC 1, E4, Radio 2 and Radio 1, focusing on the different target audiences.
- Remind learners of Stuart Hall's audience reception theory of encoding and decoding meanings (http://www.bbc.co.uk/education/guides/zg24frd/revision/3).
- Select a controversial news story open to different interpretations, such as the debate over whether women should be forced to wear high heels at work (https://www.theguardian.com/uk-news/2017/jan/25/law-must-be-tougher-over-dress-code-discrimination-say-mps).
- Ask learners to write down their reading of the news story.

Learner activities

- Learners analyse and compare the homepages of BBC 1, E4, Radio 2 and Radio 1. Are their target audiences mass or niche?
- As a class, learners discuss whether they accept the preferred reading of a controversial news article or take a negotiated or oppositional position.

Suggested homework

Learners research a news story or television/radio programme which has provoked contrasting audience responses.

Year 1 Week 6a

Introduction to music videos – media language

Learning objectives – learners will be able to:

- compare and contrast the media language styles of music videos from different musical genres
- state the codes and conventions of the music video as a media form.

Introduction

The work on music videos relates to Section A: Music for the assessment Music and News (02), the written exam paper. This could also be useful for Creating Media (03/04), the non-exam assessment. Learners need to study the set music videos in relation to media language, media representations and media audiences.

Key products

Queen, *Bohemian Rhapsody* (https://www.youtube.com/watch?v=fJ9rUzIMcZQ)

P!nk, *What About Us* (http://www.bigtop40.com/songs/pink-what-about-us/#f1rck HB4DSJqoHXF.97)

Ed Sheeran, *Shape of You* (http://www.bigtop40.com/songs/ed-sheeran-shape-of-you/# MgzJ1rOXEb0v6OC5.97)

Teacher activities

- Recap key media audience terms, including: target audience, marketing, technologies, active audiences, uses and gratifications, and changing audience responses.
- Introduce the area of study and put it into the context of the examination. A historical starting point could be Queen's *Bohemian Rhapsody*. Give learners a list of key media language terms for music videos, including: narrative, mise-en-scène, camerawork, editing, soundtrack and intertextuality.
- Screen a selection of music videos from a range of popular music genres for whole-class analysis (e.g. P!nk's *What About Us* and Ed Sheeran's *Shape of You*). Discuss how the style fits the genre and the artist, allowing learners to use media language (e.g. elements and connotations).
- Direct whole-class analysis and discussion of the music videos, encouraging learners to try out media language terms (e.g. codes and conventions, intertextuality).

Learner activities

- As a class, learners discuss and analyse what the music videos have in common (e.g. mostly non-diegetic sound, fast-paced editing, energetic camerawork, performance to camera, fictional narrative driven by performance). It may be helpful to give them a table to aid their analysis.
- Learners contribute to class feedback using the notes they have made.

Suggested homework

Learners write up their media language analysis of one of the music videos from the lesson.

Year 1 Week 6b

Introduction to music videos – representations and social group

> ### Learning objectives – learners will be able to:
>
> - analyse how music videos use media language to create connotations that fit the artists' images
> - analyse how music videos use representations to fit the artists' images
> - discuss which social groups are under-represented or misrepresented in music videos.

Key products

Robin Thicke feat. T.I. & Pharrell, *Blurred Lines*, by Robin Thicke feat. T.I. & Pharrell (https://vimeo.com/75901884)

New Music Videos, The Vodafone Big Top 40 (http://www.bigtop40.com/music-videos/)

Additional resources

YouTube Popular Music Videos (https://www.youtube.com/playlist?list=PLFgquLnL59alCl_2TQvOiD5Vgm1hCaGSI)

Music videos on Vimeo (https://vimeo.com/categories/music)

Teacher activities

- Recap (perhaps using a brief quiz) the key media language terms for music videos from the previous session, checking learners' understanding. Reinforce key terms.
- Direct whole-class analysis and discussion on connotation and artist's image, encouraging learners to try out media language terms (e.g. codes and conventions, intertextuality).
- Display how music videos use representations to fit the artist's image. Examples could be taken from New Music Videos on The Vodafone Big Top 40 website. Learners should take notes following set questions.

Learner activities

- Using computers and making notes, learners research and analyse how music videos use media language to create connotations that fit the artists' images. They could use the New Music Videos on The Vodafone Big Top 40 website. It may be helpful to give them a list of questions to aid their analysis.
- In small groups, learners discuss and make notes on which social groups are under-represented or misrepresented in music videos, including the objectification of women. They could use *Blurred Lines* by Robin Thicke feat. T.I. & Pharrell as an example.
- Learners feed back their findings to the whole class.

Suggested homework

Learners view at least three videos from genres with which they are not familiar and log whether or not they fit the conventions of music videos as a form.

Year 1 Week 7a

Set music videos – media language

Learning objectives – learners will be able to:

● compare and contrast the camerawork in the two chosen videos

● compare and contrast the editing in the two chosen videos.

Key products

Learners need to study **one set pair** of music videos from the list below:

1. **Wheatus,** *Teenage Dirtbag* (https://www.youtube.com/watch?v=FC3y9llDXuM) and **Avril Lavigne,** *Sk8er Boi* (https://www.youtube.com/watch?v=Tly3n2b7V9k)

2. **Mark Ronson feat. Bruno Mars,** *Uptown Funk* (https://www.youtube.com/watch?v=OPf0YbXqDm0) and **Beyoncé,** *If I Were A Boy* (https://www.youtube.com/watch?v=AWpsOqh8q0M)

3. **The Vamps feat. Demi Lovato,** *Somebody To You* (https://www.youtube.com/watch?v=0go2nfVXFgA) and **Little Mix,** *Black Magic* (https://www.youtube.com/watch?v=MkElfR_NPBI)

4. **Tinie Tempah feat. Jess Glynne,** *Not Letting Go* (https://www.youtube.com/watch?v=nsDwItoNlLc) and **Paloma Faith,** *Picking Up the Pieces* (https://www.youtube.com/watch?v=Ijel4Vcqd9g)

Teacher activities

● Recap key media language terms for music videos from previous lesson, including: intertextuality, narrative, camerawork, editing, mise-en-scène and soundtrack. A multiple-choice quiz could be used for this activity.

● Screen the first set music video for whole-class analysis, focusing on camerawork and editing.

● Direct whole-class analysis and discussion of the first set music video, encouraging learners to try out and apply technical terms.

Learner activities

● As a class, learners discuss and analyse the media language of the first set music video, learning to apply the correct terminology.

● In small groups, learners compare and contrast the second set music video, making observations on camerawork and editing. It may be helpful to give them a table to aid their analysis.

● Learners feed back their findings on the second set music video to the whole class.

Suggested homework

Learners write up their camerawork and editing analysis of set music videos from the lesson.

Year 1 Week 7b

Set music videos – media language

> ### Learning objectives – learners will be able to:
> - compare and contrast the use of mise-en-scène in the two chosen videos
> - compare and contrast the use (if any) of diegetic sound in the two chosen videos
> - state any use of intertextuality in the chosen videos.

Key products

Learners need to study **one set pair** of music videos from the list below:

1. **Wheatus,** *Teenage Dirtbag* (https://www.youtube.com/watch?v=FC3y9llDXuM) and **Avril Lavigne,** *Sk8er Boi* (https://www.youtube.com/watch?v=TIy3n2b7V9k)

2. **Mark Ronson feat. Bruno Mars,** *Uptown Funk* (https://www.youtube.com/watch?v=OPf0YbXqDm0) and **Beyoncé,** *If I Were A Boy* (https://www.youtube.com/watch?v=AWpsOqh8q0M)

3. **The Vamps feat. Demi Lovato,** *Somebody To You* (https://www.youtube.com/watch?v=0go2nfVXFgA) and **Little Mix,** *Black Magic* (https://www.youtube.com/watch?v=MkElfR_NPBI)

4. **Tinie Tempah feat. Jess Glynne,** *Not Letting Go* (https://www.youtube.com/watch?v=nsDwltoNlLc) and **Paloma Faith,** *Picking Up the Pieces* (https://www.youtube.com/watch?v=Ijel4Vcqd9g)

Teacher activities

- Give learners a definition of intertextuality and ask them to list examples in music videos.
- Screen the first set music video for whole-class analysis, focusing on the use of mise-en-scène, diegetic sound and intertextuality.
- Direct whole-class analysis and discussion of the set music videos, encouraging learners to try out and apply technical terms.
- Summarise media language comparison and contrast of the set music videos (recapping camerawork and editing).

Learner activities

- In small groups, learners list and feed back intertextuality examples in music videos to the class.
- In pairs, learners compare and contrast the second set music video, making notes on the use of mise-en-scène, diegetic sound and intertextuality. It may be helpful to give them a table to aid their analysis.
- Learners feed back their findings on the second set music video to the whole class.

Suggested homework

Learners write an essay in response to the question: 'How do the two music videos you have studied use media language in the same way and differently?'

Year 1 Week 8a

Set music videos – media representations

> ### Learning objectives – learners will be able to:
> - compare and contrast the social groups represented in the two chosen videos
> - compare and contrast the use of stereotypes (or anti-stereotypes) in the two chosen videos.

Key products

Learners need to study **one set pair** of music videos from the list below:

1. **Wheatus, *Teenage Dirtbag*** (https://www.youtube.com/watch?v=FC3y9llDXuM) and **Avril Lavigne, *Sk8er Boi*** (https://www.youtube.com/watch?v=Tly3n2b7V9k)

2. **Mark Ronson feat. Bruno Mars, *Uptown Funk*** (https://www.youtube.com/watch?v=OPf0YbXqDm0) and **Beyoncé, *If I Were A Boy*** (https://www.youtube.com/watch?v=AWpsOqh8q0M)

3. **The Vamps feat. Demi Lovato, *Somebody To You*** (https://www.youtube.com/watch?v=0go2nfVXFgA) and **Little Mix, *Black Magic*** (https://www.youtube.com/watch?v=MkElfR_NPBI)

4. **Tinie Tempah feat. Jess Glynne, *Not Letting Go*** (https://www.youtube.com/watch?v=nsDwItoNlLc) and **Paloma Faith, *Picking Up the Pieces*** (https://www.youtube.com/watch?v=Ijel4Vcqd9g)

Teacher activities

- Recap media language comparison and contrast in set music videos (e.g. camerawork, editing, use of mise-en-scène, use of diegetic sound and intertextuality).
- Screen the second set music video for whole-class analysis, focusing on the social group's representation and the use of stereotypes (or anti-stereotypes).
- Direct whole-class analysis and discussion of the set music videos, encouraging learners to try out and apply the key terms.

Learner activities

- As a class, learners discuss and analyse media representation of the second set music video, learning to apply the correct terminology.
- In pairs, learners compare and contrast the first set music video, making notes on the social group's representation and the use of stereotypes (or anti-stereotypes). It may be helpful to give them a table to aid their analysis.
- Learners feed back their findings on the first set music video to the whole class.

Suggested homework

Learners write up their media representation analysis of set music videos from the lesson.

Year 1 Week 8b

Set music videos – media representations

Learning objectives – learners will be able to:

- compare and contrast the messages and values in the two chosen videos.

Key products

Learners need to study **one set pair** of music videos from the list below:

1. **Wheatus, *Teenage Dirtbag*** (https://www.youtube.com/watch?v=FC3y9llDXuM) and **Avril Lavigne, *Sk8er Boi*** (https://www.youtube.com/watch?v=Tly3n2b7V9k)

2. **Mark Ronson feat. Bruno Mars, *Uptown Funk*** (https://www.youtube.com/watch?v=OPf0YbXqDm0) and **Beyoncé, *If I Were A Boy*** (https://www.youtube.com/watch?v=AWpsOqh8q0M)

3. **The Vamps feat. Demi Lovato, *Somebody To You*** (https://www.youtube.com/watch?v=0go2nfVXFgA) and **Little Mix, *Black Magic*** (https://www.youtube.com/watch?v=MkElfR_NPBI)

4. **Tinie Tempah feat. Jess Glynne, *Not Letting Go*** (https://www.youtube.com/watch?v=nsDwltoNlLc) and **Paloma Faith, *Picking Up the Pieces*** (https://www.youtube.com/watch?v=Ijel4Vcqd9g)

Teacher activities

- Recap media representations elements from the previous session.
- Direct whole-class analysis and discussion of the set music videos, encouraging learners to try out and apply the key terms. Focus on messages and values.
- Set a timed writing exercise.
- Learners could focus on differences in media representation (e.g. *Sk8ter Boi* celebrates teenage rebellion and rule-breaking, whereas *Teenage Dirtbag* represents a character trying to conform and succeed, and the highly individualistic, status-ridden and competitive world in *Teenage Dirtbag* contrasts with the solidarity of an outsider community in *Sk8ter Boi*).
- Facilitate review discussion of the set music videos. Learners will revisit the set music videos in Year 2 Week 15.

Learner activities

- In pairs, learners compare and contrast the set music videos, making notes on messages and values. It may be helpful to give them a list of questions to aid their analysis.
- Learners feed back their findings on the set music videos to the whole class.
- Learners complete a timed writing activity: 'Compare and contrast apparent media representations from the set music videos.'

Suggested homework

Learners view other music videos by the same artists. They should make notes on media representations.

Year 1 Week 9a

Introduction to magazines – codes and conventions

> ### Learning objectives – learners will be able to:
> ● state the codes and conventions of the magazine as a media form.

Introduction

The work on magazines relates to Section A: Music for the assessment Music and News (02), the written exam paper. This could also be useful for Creating Media (03/04), the non-exam assessment. Learners must study magazine set products in relation to all four areas of the media theoretical framework (media language, media representations, media industries and media audiences), including all relevant theoretical approaches and social and cultural contexts.

Key products

The Week Junior **magazine** (http://theweekjunior.co.uk/)

Cosmopolitan **magazine** (http://www.hearstmagazines.co.uk/co/cosmopolitan-magazine-subscription-website?utm_source=cosmopolitan.co.uk&utm_medium=referral&utm_content=nav-bar)

SciFiNow **magazine** (https://www.scifinow.co.uk/)

The History of Magazines (https://www.magazines.com/history-of-magazines)

Teacher activities

● Recap media representation comparison and contrast of the set music videos (e.g. social groups represented, the use of stereotypes or anti-stereotypes, and the messages and values).

● Introduce the area of study and put it into the context of the examination.

● Give learners a list of key media language terms for magazines, including: masthead, cover lines, cover image, layout, typography, images and graphics, use of colour.

● Display a variety of magazine front covers from different genres (e.g. current affairs, lifestyle and special interest) for whole-class analysis, focusing on the codes and conventions of the magazine as a form. The magazines could include *The Week Junior*, *Cosmopolitan* and *SciFiNow*.

● Direct whole-class analysis and discussion of magazine front covers and content, encouraging learners to try out and apply the codes and conventions key terms.

Learner activities

● As a class, learners discuss and analyse what the magazine front covers have in common (e.g. masthead, cover lines, cover image).

● Learners contribute to class feedback using the notes they have made.

Suggested homework

Learners write an essay in response to the question: 'Write an analysis of one of the front covers discussed in class, using the correct media terminology.'

Year 1 Week 9b

Introduction to music magazines

Learning objectives – learners will be able to:

- compare and contrast the media language styles of music magazines from different musical genres
- state the generic codes and conventions of the music magazine.

Key products

Music magazines front covers (https://www.pinterest.co.uk/pin/402087072953534955/)

Additional resources

BBC Bitesize – GCSE Media Studies – Magazines (http://www.bbc.co.uk/education/guides/zcpgdmn/revision)

BBC Bitesize – GCSE Media Studies – Industries overview (http://www.bbc.co.uk/education/guides/zqrdxsg/revision)

Teacher activities

- Introduce music magazines as an area of study in the context of the examination.
- Facilitate whole-class analysis and discussion of music magazines (front covers and content) from different musical genres, encouraging learners to try out and apply the codes and conventions key terms. You could use the 'Music magazines front covers' Pinterest page.
- Recap the generic codes and conventions of music magazines, writing a list on the board.

Learner activities

- Learners view music magazines from different musical genres. They make notes on the similarities and differences in media language styles.
- In small groups, learners analyse and compare at least three music magazine front covers (making notes) and list generic conventions (e.g. image of musician/s on front cover, genre of music, addressing fandom for a musical genre tone). It may be helpful to give learners a table to aid their analysis.
- Learners record the board work on the generic codes and conventions of music magazines in their exercise books.
- Learners contribute to class feedback using their notes.

Suggested homework

Learners write up their media language analysis of one of the magazines from the lesson.

Year 1 Week 10a

Music magazine – media language

Learning objectives – learners will be able to:

- analyse *MOJO* front covers in terms of layout, typography, image, graphics, colour and language use
- suggest how this media language addresses a mature, mostly male audience of fans of 'classic rock'
- state the main features of the house style of the whole magazine.

Key products

Centres need at least two magazines so that learners can study one whole edition and at least two covers.

MOJO magazine

Q magazine or music magazine alternative

Additional resources

MOJO magazine homepage (http://www.mojo4music.com/)

MOJO magazine latest issue and cover archive (http://www.mojo4music.com/magazine/)

Q magazine homepage (http://www.qthemusic.com/)

The latest Q magazine (https://www.qthemusic.com/the-latest-issue/)

Teacher activities

- Recap key media language terms for magazines, including: masthead, cover lines, cover image, layout, typography, images and graphics, use of colour.
- Display the *MOJO* magazine front cover and content for whole-class analysis, focusing on media language (e.g. layout, typography, image, graphics, colour and language use).
- Direct whole-class analysis and discussion of the *MOJO* magazine front cover and content (e.g. addresses a mature, mostly male audience of fans of 'classic rock'), encouraging learners to try out and apply the key terms.

Learner activities

- As a class, learners discuss and analyse media language in relation to *MOJO* magazine's house style, learning to apply the correct terminology.
- In pairs, learners compare and contrast the *MOJO* magazine front cover and content with *Q* magazine, making notes on media language. It may be helpful to give them a table to aid their analysis.
- Learners contribute to class feedback using their notes.

Suggested homework

Learners write up their media language analysis of *MOJO* magazine from the lesson.

Year 1 Week 10b

Music magazine – media language

Learning objectives – learners will be able to:

- state how two regular features in the magazine address the target audience
- state any use of intertextuality in the magazine.

Key products

Centres need at least two magazines so that learners can study one whole edition and at least two covers.

MOJO magazine

Q magazine or music magazine alternative

Additional resources

MOJO magazine homepage (http://www.mojo4music.com/)

MOJO magazine latest issue and cover archive (http://www.mojo4music.com/magazine/)

Q magazine homepage (http://www.qthemusic.com/)

The latest Q magazine (https://www.qthemusic.com/the-latest-issue/)

Teacher activities

- Display *MOJO* magazine for whole-class analysis, focusing on the target audience. Show the front cover and content throughout the magazine. Focus on at least two regular features.
- Give learners a definition of intertextuality and ask them to find examples in music magazines.
- Direct whole-class analysis and discussion of *MOJO* magazine, encouraging learners to try out and apply the key terms.

Learner activities

- In small groups, learners search for intertextuality examples in music magazines, making notes in their exercise books.
- As a class, learners discuss and analyse intertextuality in music magazines, learning to apply the correct terminology.
- In pairs, learners compare and contrast the *MOJO* magazine front cover and content with *Q* magazine, making notes on audience address. It may be helpful to give them a table to aid their analysis.
- Learners feed back their findings to the whole class.

Suggested homework

Learners pick one other music magazine and note how the layout, typography, images and graphics, use of colour and language differ from those of *MOJO*.

Year 1 Week 11a

Music magazine – media representations

Learning objectives – learners will be able to:

- analyse the social groups present in and absent from *MOJO* magazine
- discuss the reasons for this presence/absence
- discuss the use of stereotypes (and/or anti-stereotypes) in *MOJO* magazine – especially gender stereotypes.

Key products

Centres need at least two magazines so that learners can study one whole edition and at least two covers.

***MOJO* magazine**

***Q* magazine** or music magazine alternative

Teacher activities

- Recap media language comparison and contrast of two magazine front covers and content (including *MOJO*), including layout, typography, image, graphics, colour and language use.
- Display *MOJO* magazine for whole-class analysis, focusing on the choices media producers made about how to represent social groups and stereotyping (and/or anti-stereotyping). Learners should take notes during the analysis.
- Direct whole-class analysis and discussion of two magazines' front covers and content (including *MOJO*), encouraging learners to try out and apply the representation and audience key terms (e.g. reasons for presence and absence).

Learner activities

- As a class, learners discuss and analyse media representation in *MOJO* magazine, learning to apply the correct terminology.
- In pairs, learners compare and contrast *MOJO* magazine with *Q* magazine, making notes on media representations. Focus should be on gender stereotypes.
- Using computers, learners investigate and research whether the content of two music magazines excludes social groups based on gender, age, sexuality and race/ethnicity. It may be helpful to give them a list of questions to aid their research.
- Learners feed back their findings on *MOJO* magazine and *Q* magazine to the whole class.

Suggested homework

Learners write up their media representation analysis of *MOJO* magazine from the lesson.

Year 1 Week 11b

Music magazine – media representations and audiences

Learning objectives – learners will be able to:

- analyse the messages and values in *MOJO* magazine
- suggest how these representations address a mature, mostly male audience of fans of 'classic rock'.

Key products

Centres need at least two magazines so that learners can study one whole edition and at least two covers.

MOJO magazine

Q magazine or music magazine alternative

Additional resources

MOJO magazine homepage (http://www.mojo4music.com/)

MOJO magazine latest issue and cover archive (http://www.mojo4music.com/magazine/)

Q magazine homepage (http://www.qthemusic.com/)

The latest Q magazine (https://www.qthemusic.com/the-latest-issue/)

Teacher activities

- Display *Q* magazine for whole-class analysis, focusing on the messages, values and beliefs conveyed, and the significance of the representations in terms of the themes or issues addressed.
- Direct whole-class analysis and discussion of two magazines' front covers and content (including *MOJO*), encouraging learners to try out and apply the representation and audience key terms.
- Facilitate review discussion of music magazines.
- Learners will revisit the set magazine in Year 2 Week 16.

Learner activities

- As a class, learners discuss and analyse media representation in *Q* magazine, learning to apply the correct terminology.
- In pairs, learners compare and contrast *Q* magazine with *MOJO* magazine, making notes on media representation and audience (e.g. address a mature, mostly male audience of fans of 'classic rock').
- Using computers, learners investigate and research the messages and values in *MOJO* magazine. It may be helpful to give them a list of questions to aid their research.
- Learners feed back their findings on *MOJO* magazine to the whole class.

Suggested homework

Learners pick one other music magazine and note how the representations differ from those of *MOJO*.

Year 1 Week 12a

Television – crime drama

Learning objectives – learners will be able to:

● state the generic codes and conventions of crime drama

● exemplify how *Cuffs* fits crime drama codes and conventions

● analyse how *Cuffs* creates ongoing multiple storylines based on the 'everyday life' of a police station.

Key product

Cuffs, Series 1, Episode 1, BBC1 (available on DVD)

Teacher activities

● Introduce the area of study and put it into the context of the examination.

● Lead a brief class recap of the codes and conventions of television crime drama from lessons 3a and 3b.

● Provide contextual background to the programme, including main character names, a brief overview of the narrative being established and where the episode is set.

● Divide learners into groups of four and give each group a different area of focus on which to make notes during the screening. Areas on which to make notes are: storylines, including content, number of different storylines, whether they are concluded or continue to the next episode; and character, including the number of characters, their gender, ethnicity, position in the narrative (lead or supporting character) and anything else significant.

● Screen the whole episode of *Cuffs* (1 hour duration).

Learner activities

● In pairs, learners will make detailed notes on their assigned area during the screening of the episode, in preparation for discussion work in next lesson.

Suggested homework

Learners watch one other crime drama and note similar or different use of conventions.

Year 1 Week 12b

Television – crime drama

Learning objectives – learners will be able to:

- exemplify how *Cuffs* fits crime drama codes and conventions
- analyse how *Cuffs* creates ongoing multiple storylines based on the 'everyday life' of a police station.
- discuss how successfully *Cuffs* creates a social realism like that of a soap opera
- state how broadcast television as a technology suits serial narratives (e.g. as compared with film).

Key products

Cuffs, Series 1, Episode 1, BBC1

Radio Times television schedule: http://www.radiotimes.com/tv/tv-listings/

Teacher activities

- Lead a recap of the narrative of the episode of *Cuffs* watched in lesson 12a.
- Organise learners into groups of four – two who have made notes on storylines and two who have made notes on character.
- Direct each group of learners to create a narrative arc (using a graph or axis) to identify which storylines are completed and which continue. Note on the arc which characters are involved in each storyline, the theme of the storyline and when they appear and disappear during the episode. (Learners will use these arcs again in lesson 14b.)
- Facilitate feedback on a class discussion on narrative and storylines in crime drama and how storylines are based on the 'everyday' life of the police station. Discuss differences between series and serials, referring to storylines to illustrate this.
- Lead a comparison between the nature of the storylines in *Cuffs* and those found in other television programmes such as soap operas. Ask learners to consider why we believe these storylines to be 'real'.
- Project a page from the weekly television schedules. Direct learners to identify which programmes are series and which are serials. Discuss why schedules are built around these kinds of programmes.

Learner activities

- In groups, learners create a narrative arc to plot the storylines in the episode of *Cuffs* watched in lesson 12a.
- Learners contribute to a class discussion focused on narrative content and its links to real life.
- Learners identify examples of series and serials from the television schedules.

Suggested homework

Learners write a review of a television crime drama.

Year 1 Week 13a

Television – crime drama

> ## Learning objectives – learners will be able to:
>
> - analyse the camerawork in sequences from *Cuffs*
> - analyse the soundtrack in sequences from *Cuffs*.

Key products

Cuffs, Series 1, Episode 1, BBC1

Cuffs, Series 1, Episode 7, BBC1

Teacher activities

- Test learners' understanding of key media terms of camerawork and sound through a quiz (Kahoot! or Socrative, if available) or timed brainstorm using large sheets of sugar paper. Get learners to write down as many different terms as they can remember in 2 minutes.
- Choose four camerawork terms and four sound terms and ask individual learners to explain what the terms mean through targeted questioning.
- Screen the opening sequence to *Cuffs*, Series 1, Episode 7, three times. Pause after the first screening for a brief discussion with learners about which conventions are established in the opening. Leave a gap of 2 minutes between screening 2 and 3 for note-making.
- Direct half the class to make notes on how camerawork creates meaning and the remaining half on how sound creates meaning.
- Facilitate feedback in small groups.
- Screen a second sequence, this time from Series 1, Episode 1.
- Direct learners to individually analyse how both camerawork and sound create meaning.

Learner activities

- Learners demonstrate knowledge of key terms of camerawork and sound through the quiz.
- Learners make notes on either camerawork or sound during the screenings.
- Learners share their feedback with another learner who explored the same area, and then share their feedback with a learner who looked at a different area.
- Learners make notes on both camerawork and sound in the second sequence.

Year 1 Week 13b

Television – crime drama

Learning objectives – learners will be able to:

- analyse the mise-en-scène in sequences from *Cuffs*
- analyse the editing in sequences from *Cuffs*.
- state any use of intertextuality in the sequences.

Key products

Cuffs, Series 1, Episode 1, BBC1

Cuffs, Series 1, Episode 7, BBC1

Teacher activities

- Lead revision of mise-en-scène and editing terms: display definitions of the terms and ask learners to match the terms to the definitions.
- Screen the opening sequence to Series 1, Episode 7, of *Cuffs* once and then screen your chosen sequence from Series 1, Episode 1.
- Direct learners to identify four uses of mise-en-scène and four uses of editing in creating effect.
- Facilitate feedback discussion focusing on how meaning is created, making notes on the board.
- Set the timed writing activity below.

Learner activities

- Learners match definitions to terms.
- Individually, learners identify four uses of mise-en-scène and four uses of editing that create meaning.
- Learners share their observations with the class.
- Learners complete a timed writing activity, answering the following question: 'How is media language used to create meaning in the opening sequence?'

Suggested homework

Learners research reviews of *Cuffs*. They summarise how the programme was received by both critics and audiences.

Year 1 Week 14a

Television – crime drama

Learning objectives – learners will be able to:

- analyse the social groups present in and absent from *Cuffs*
- discuss reasons for the presence/absence of these representations in *Cuffs*
- discuss the use of stereotypes (and/or anti-stereotypes) in *Cuffs* – especially gender stereotypes.

Key products

Cuffs, Series 1, Episode 1, BBC1

Cuffs, Series 1, Episode 7 , BBC1

If possible, prepare digitised sequences from the key episode for student access in class.

Teacher activities

- Lead a recap on stereotypes, anti-stereotypes and gender stereotypes.
- Screen the opening sequence to *Cuffs*, Series 1, Episode 7, once to revise.
- Ask learners briefly to identify any obvious stereotypes or anti-stereotypes found within the first five minutes. How, in particular, is gender represented?
- Screen a second sequence of your choice from Series 1, Episode 1.
- Ask learners to create a character list, identifying elements including gender, ethnicity, age range and other relevant social groups. They should do this individually and feed back as a jigsaw exercise.
- Lead a discussion around which social groups or stereotypes are absent, being challenged and being reinforced. Encourage learners to consider reasons why this may be so.
- Assign pairs or threes a character and ask learners to identify and present one other key sequence from the episode of *Cuffs* which either challenges or conforms to expected stereotypes.

Learner activities

- Learners make notes to recap their understanding of stereotypes.
- Learners identify at least one stereotype and one anti-stereotype found in the opening sequence of *Cuffs*, Series 1, Episode 7.
- Learners build a profile of their assigned character or characters. They present their profiles to the rest of the class.
- In pairs or threes, learners identify a second sequence from the episode which demonstrates stereotypes being conformed to or challenged, and present this sequence to the class.

Year 1 Week 14b

Television – crime drama

Learning objectives – learners will be able to:

- analyse the messages and values in *Cuffs*
- make suggestions as to how representations found in the programme address a mainstream mass audience.

Key products

Cuffs, Series 1, Episode 1, BBC1

Cuffs, Series 1, Episode 7, BBC1

Teacher activities

- Lead a short recap of audience types, revising lessons 5a and 5b.
- Place learners into small groups of three or four and assign each group a different character from the chosen episode.
- Ask learners to refer back to their narrative arc created in lesson 12b. Add to this arc, in a different colour, by identifying the messages and values communicated by the storylines.
- Using this information, introduce a class discussion focusing on the messages and values found within the episode based on the characters and their relationship with the narrative and storylines.
- Ask learners to write a short paragraph that identifies which messages and values of the episode would meet the needs of a mainstream mass audience.

Learner activities

- Learners create a visual narrative map of the action and activities in which their assigned character is involved.
- Learners contribute to a class discussion around messages and values found within the episode.
- Learners write approximately 100 words on which message and values found within the episode would appeal to a mainstream mass audience.

Suggested homework

Bringing together learning from lessons 14a and 14b, learners answer the following question: 'How do the representations and media language found in *Cuffs* try to engage a mass audience?'

Year 1 Week 15a

Promoting media – film

Learning objectives – learners will be able to:

- analyse *The Lego Movie* posters in terms of layout, typography, image, graphics, colour and language use
- compare and contrast the character posters.

Key products

The Lego Movie **UK TV trailer:** https://www.youtube.com/watch?v=HSbYBzUEQlc

The Lego Movie **poster campaign:**

1. The main poster featuring an ensemble cast, running from danger (http://www.impawards. com/2014/lego_movie_ver9.html)

2. Character poster of Vitruvius in close-up (http://www.impawards.com/2014/lego_movie_ver3. html)

3. Character poster of Emmet in close-up (http://www.impawards.com/2014/lego_movie_ver8. html)

4. Character poster of Lord Business in close-up (http://www.impawards.com/2014/lego_movie_ ver5.html)

5. Character poster of Wyldstyle in close-up (http://www.impawards.com/2014/lego_movie_ ver7.html)

Teacher activities

- Give learners a black and white copy of *The Lego Movie* poster (ensemble cast) and ask them in pairs to predict how colour is used in the colour version (see below).
- Display the colour poster and direct whole-class analysis of the colour choices that learners predicted, focusing on and comparing the actual colours used in the poster.
- Introduce media language elements and reinforce the use of connotative analysis.
- Display the ensemble poster and lead a group discussion of layout, encouraging learners to annotate a personal colour copy of the poster.
- Facilitate the group task, allocating each group a character poster to analyse.
- Encourage learners to focus on the differences between the character posters.

Learner activities

- In pairs, learners discuss and record their expectations of the use of colour for their own selection of key elements in the poster.
- In groups, learners analyse their allocated character poster in terms of typography, image, graphics and language use.
- In their groups, learners feed back their findings to the whole class.
- Individually, learners take notes on how the posters differ from one another.

Suggested homework

Learners select a character poster and annotate it with analysis of layout and colour.

Year 1 Week 15b

Promoting media – film

Learning objectives – learners will be able to:

- analyse examples of camerawork, editing, mise-en-scène and soundtrack in *The Lego Movie*
- identify and analyse any use of intertextuality in *The Lego Movie* posters and trailer.

Key products

The Lego Movie **UK TV trailer:** https://www.youtube.com/watch?v=HSbYBzUEQlc

The Lego Movie **poster campaign:** as per Week 15a

The Lego Movie **video game walkthroughs:** http://uk.ign.com/wikis/the-lego-movie-video-game/Prologue_-_The_Prophecy

Teacher activities

- Ask learners to reflect on their personal experience of film advertising.
- Facilitate a group feedback session, establish the key requirements for successful film trailers.
- Introduce the concept of intertextuality (perhaps display a still shot from the trailer 'A popular band' poster 1:12 to use as a discussion point, or use this link: http://www.worshipthebrand.com/gallery/item/13-graphic-design/775-a-popular-band-poster).
- Screen *The Lego Movie* trailer and provide film posters from the previous lesson.
- Divide learners into groups focusing on camerawork, editing, mise-en-scène or soundtrack. Ask them to reflect in detail on how the media language element is used to promote the film. Facilitate the production of analytical paragraphs.

Learner activities

- In pairs, learners discuss any film trailers they can recall which have either successfully promoted a film to encourage them to watch it at the cinema or discouraged them from wanting to see a film.
- In pairs, learners agree some key requirements of a successful film trailer.
- As a class, learners watch the trailer, noting any 'recognisable' characters, music, logos/brands. They feed back and discuss, referring to film posters in conjunction with the trailer. Ensure that they have a working definition of intertextuality.
- As a class, learners watch the trailer again, making notes on camerawork, editing, mise-en-scène or soundtrack.
- In small groups, learners prepare a paragraph explaining how their media language element is used effectively to promote the film. They exchange and review another group's paragraph, amending and editing if necessary. They agree final paragraphs and swap.

Suggested homework

Learners watch a walkthrough for *The Lego Movie* game. They prepare five still shots to present to the class, introducing them to the selection.

Year 1 Week 16a

Promoting media – film

Learning objectives – learners will be able to:

- analyse the social groups present in and absent from the advertising for *The Lego Movie*
- discuss the reasons for this presence/absence
- discuss the use of stereotypes (and/or anti-stereotypes) in the advertising for *The Lego Movie* – especially gender- and age-related stereotypes.

Key products

The Lego Movie **UK TV trailer:** https://www.youtube.com/watch?v=HSbYBzUEQlc

The Lego Movie **poster campaign:**

1. The main poster featuring an ensemble cast, running from danger (http://www.impawards. com/2014/lego_movie_ver9.html)

2. Character poster of Vitruvius in close-up (http://www.impawards.com/2014/lego_movie_ver3.html)

3. Character poster of Emmet in close-up (http://www.impawards.com/2014/lego_movie_ver8.html)

4. Character poster of Lord Business in close-up (http://www.impawards.com/2014/lego_movie_ver5.html)

5. Character poster of Wyldstyle in close-up (http://www.impawards.com/2014/lego_movie_ver7.html)

Teacher activities

- Ask learners to reflect on their personal experience of film advertising, focusing on the involvement of familiar or expected social groups.
- Screen *The Lego Movie* trailer and provide film posters from the previous lesson.
- Ask learners to consider which social groups are present in the advertising materials and then evaluate which social groups are excluded. Perhaps display a range of social groups on the board as guidance.
- Challenge learners to envisage how the film advertising would be affected by the appearance of one of the excluded social groups.
- Facilitate a discussion on the reasons why films for a global market might feature a dominance of white American characters in their advertising.

Learner activities

- As a group, learners reflect on and recall a range of social groups that appears in popular films.
- In pairs, learners create a character list detailing all the characters with a role in *The Lego Movie*.
- In pairs, learners analyse which social groups are represented and divide up the characters according to the social groups they belong to. Students produce a pie chart or graph from their findings.
- As a group, learners evaluate which social group(s) appear(s) to have a dominant role in the advertising. They write a paragraph for each group revealing the messages and values that the audience receives about the members of the group from the advertising.

Suggested homework

Learners prepare a half-page essay plan on 'How far does the advertising for *The Lego Movie* use stereotypes?'.

Year 1 Week 16b

Promoting media – film

Learning objectives – learners will be able to:

- discuss the use of stereotypes (and/or anti-stereotypes) in the advertising for *The Lego Movie* – especially gender- and age-related stereotypes
- analyse the messages and values in the advertising for *The Lego Movie.*

Key products

***The Lego Movie* UK TV trailer:** https://www.youtube.com/watch?v=HSbYBzUEQlc

***The Lego Movie* poster campaign:** as per Week 16a

Teacher activities

- Provide a range of images depicting accepted gender- and age-based stereotypes.
- Provide a range of images depicting disability (perhaps Ellie Simmonds or Steven Hawking), age, race.
- Screen *The Lego Movie* trailer and provide film posters from the previous lesson.
- Display large images of Wyldstyle and Vitruvius; facilitate a discussion posing the hypothesis that these characters could be gender role reversed.
- Select and screen clips of Wyldstyle and Vitruvius in action. If possible, provide transcripts to accompany the visuals.

Learner activities

- Learners look at the images and clips and discuss what they reveal about society's values (focus particularly on gender and age-related expectations of people). They consider which are positive and which are negative representations.
- In small groups, learners focus on what the film advertising reveals about our attitudes to heroism, gender and social control. Learners should identify what *The Lego Movie* advertising materials are asking us to celebrate or criticise in our culture.
- In groups, learners compare the images of Wyldstyle and Vitruvius. They agree five ways that the characters conform to our expectations of stereotypes. They identify elements of the poster and the trailer that depict anti-stereotypical qualities for these characters.
- In pairs, learners consider the experience and effects the different methods of advertising have on audiences. They produce a table of the benefits and disadvantages offered by the different print and audio-visual technologies when advertising a film.

Suggested homework

Learners write a 500-word essay: 'How far does the advertising for *The Lego Movie* use stereotypes?'

Year 1 Week 17a

Online news – media language and audience address

Learning objectives – learners will be able to:

- analyse *The Observer* homepage in terms of layout, typography, image, graphics, colour and language use, and functionality
- suggest how this media language addresses a mixed-gender, mature, middle-class, 'progressive' audience
- state any use of intertextuality in *The Observer* homepage.

Key product

***Observer* homepage:** http://www.theguardian.com/observer

Teacher activities

- Give learners a list of key terms and their definitions for online analysis, including: layout, typography, functionality, colour, language, denotation, connotation, messages, values (see the glossary at the end of these resources).
- Direct whole-class analysis and discussion of the homepage.
- Through whole-group discussion, construct an ideal type of the 'mature, middle-class, progressive' audience in terms of their lifestyle, politics and other media use.
- Explain what this audience might be expected to demand from their media products (e.g. sophistication, depth, wit, liberal political attitudes) and set the task to seek evidence of this from the homepage.

Learner activities

- As a class, learners discuss and analyse the online *Observer* homepage, learning to apply the correct terminology and including any use of intertextuality.
- In pairs, learners analyse the homepage in terms of its audience address.
- Learners feed back their findings to the whole class.

Suggested homework

Learners read one opinion piece and one review, including some of the comments.

Year 1 Week 17b

Online news – media language and audience address

Learning objectives – learners will be able to:

- state the main features of the house style from *The Observer* homepage that are continued through the website
- state how two regular sections on the website address a mixed-gender, mature, middle-class, 'progressive' audience
- state any use of intertextuality in *The Observer* website
- discuss how the online newspaper uses digital technology.

Key product

Observer **homepage:** http://www.theguardian.com/observer

Teacher activities

- Review the homepage analysis and the nature of a 'mature, middle-class, progressive' audience.
- Set the paired task below and help learners to analyse two other pages on the website.
- Direct whole-class discussion on the role of technology in the online *Observer* (e.g. immediacy – instant updating, use of hyperlinks to other articles, including archive, use of embedded video, audience interactivity via comments, opportunities for citizen journalism, links to social media and opportunities for likes and (re)tweets).

Learner activities

- In pairs, learners analyse two pages from two different sections of the website in terms of their audience address, any use of intertextuality and the key elements of the website's house style.
- Learners feed back their findings to the whole class.
- As a class, learners discuss what the online newspaper can do easily that the print one cannot.

Year 1 Week 18a

Online news and social media – media language and audience address

Learning objectives – learners will be able to:

- analyse the *Guardian* Instagram feed in terms of layout, typography, image, graphics, colour, language use and functionality
- suggest how this media language addresses the *Observer* target audience
- state any use of intertextuality in the *Guardian* Instagram feed
- discuss how the Instagram feed uses technology to allow audience participation.

Key product

Guardian **Instagram feed:** http://www.instagram.com/guardian/?hl=en

Teacher activities

- Review key terms for online analysis, including: layout, typography, functionality, colour, language, connotation, messages, values.
- Display the *Guardian* Instagram feed for whole-class analysis OR direct learners to open the Instagram feed for individual analysis.
- Direct class discussion on the opportunities for audience participation on Instagram (likes, comments, attracting followers, choosing who to follow, etc.) and collect examples of comments that do not reflect *The Observer*'s liberal viewpoint.

Learner activities

- As a class, learners discuss and analyse the *Guardian* Instagram feed, applying the correct terminology. Or learners can do individual analysis of media language elements and audience address (noting which elements are controlled by Instagram and which reflect the choices the *Guardian* has made).
- Learners note examples of intertextuality.
- Learners suggest means of audience participation on Instagram and discuss how far the *Guardian* Instagram audience might differ from that for the newspaper website.

Suggested homework

Learners follow up from last week's topic by accessing the *Mail* website and listing differences from *Observer* website.

Year 1 Week 18b

Online news and social media – media language and audience address

---

Learning objectives – learners will be able to:

- analyse the *Guardian* Twitter feed in terms of layout, typography, image, graphics, colour, language use and functionality
- suggest how this media language addresses the *Observer* target audience
- state any use of intertextuality in the *Guardian* Twitter feed
- discuss how the Twitter feed uses technology to allow audience participation.

Key product

***Guardian* Twitter feed:** https://twitter.com/guardian

Teacher activities

- Review key terms for online analysis, including: layout, typography, functionality, colour, language, connotation, messages, values.
- Display the *Guardian* Twitter feed for whole-class analysis OR direct learners to open the Twitter feed for individual analysis.
- Explain to learners that *The Guardian* and *The Observer* are both owned by the Guardian Media Group, which in turn is owned by Scott Trust Limited. The two newspapers target similar audiences. The strong links between the two newspapers mean that their Twitter and Instagram feeds are shared.
- Direct class discussion on the opportunities for audience participation on Twitter (likes, replies, retweets, attracting followers, choosing who to follow, etc.) and collect examples of replies that do or do not reflect *The Observer*'s liberal viewpoint.

Learner activities

- As a class, learners discuss and analyse the *Guardian* Twitter feed, applying the correct terminology. Or learners do individual analysis of media language elements and audience address (noting which elements are controlled by Twitter and which reflect the choices the *Guardian* has made).
- Learners note examples of intertextuality.
- Learners suggest means of audience participation on Twitter and discuss how far the *Guardian* Twitter audience might be similar to or differ from that for the newspaper website.

Suggested homework

Learners access the *Mail* online Twitter feed and list differences from the *Guardian* Twitter feed.

Year 1 Week 19a

Introduction to creating media – preliminary production

Learning objectives – learners will be able to:

- discuss how the practical production will use media language and representation to communicate meaning to an intended audience
- understand how individual research and planning will inform their own practical production.

Key products

CBeebies **magazine** (https://www.facebook.com/cbeebiesmag/)

Newsround **website** (http://www.bbc.co.uk/newsround)

Little Mix's *Black Magic* (https://www.youtube.com/watch?v=MkElfR_NPBI)

Stampy's website (http://stampysofficalwebsite.webs.com/) and **YouTube channel** (https://www.youtube.com/user/electablepanda8/channels)

Teacher activities

- Explain the Creating Media component, with its particular focus on media language, representation (including stereotypes and the ways in which representations are constructed) and intended audience. Explain that learners must work individually on this component, although they can use other learners as models, cast or crew.
- Display or screen an existing media product with a very clear use of media language to construct a particular representation for an intended audience. For example, *CBeebies* magazine, the *Newsround* website, Little Mix's *Black Magic* music video, Stampy's website and YouTube channel.
- Manage class feedback on media language, representation and intended audience.
- Set up the preliminary three-week mini production. Ask learners individually to research and plan a mini production aimed at 6–10 year olds. For example: a cover page for a new magazine; 20–30 seconds of a new TV programme or music video; a homepage for a new website. Ensure that learners plan to work in the same form that they will use for their final production, so they can practise the relevant practical skills.

Learner activities

- Learners identify the following in the exemplar media products: key uses of codes and conventions and media language; representation (including stereotypes and the ways in which representations are constructed); the intended audience.
- Learners discuss their findings as a class.
- Learners research existing media products independently in order to plan their own mini production. They record this research in a log book or a blog.

Suggested homework

Learners continue researching existing media products.

Year 1 Week 19b

Introduction to creating media – preliminary production

Learning objectives – learners will be able to:

- discuss how the practical production will use media language and representation to communicate meaning to an intended audience
- understand how to write the Statement of Intent, and its significance
- understand how individual research and planning will inform their own practical production.

Teacher activities

- Recap on the three key areas which are examined in this component.
- Explain the significance of the Statement of Intent and what needs to be included: the ways in which learners will apply their knowledge and understanding of media language and representation; how they will target their intended audience and how they have responded to their research findings (see pages 38–9 of the specification).
- Ask learners to write a brief Statement of Intent for their mini production (approximately 100–50 words), including a comment on whether they intend to use stereotypes and/or anti-stereotypes.
- Ask learners to continue researching and to begin planning their mini productions.
- Facilitate individual research and planning, ensuring that these are recorded in log books or electronically. If time allows, ask learners to prepare a one-minute pitch on their production to the whole class.

Learner activities

- Learners draft a brief Statement of Intent (around 100–150 words), including whether they intend to use stereotypes and/or anti-stereotypes.
- Learners research existing media products in order to plan their own mini production, recording their findings. They plan their own mini production, identifying locations and additional cast, crew or models. They use storyboards, mock-ups, drafts, test shots.
- Learners prepare a one-minute pitch to 'sell' their idea for the production to the rest of the class.

Suggested homework

Learners continue planning their mini productions.

Year 1 Week 20a

Introduction to creating media – preliminary production

Learning objectives – learners will be able to:

- use technology to produce a media product
- practise and develop the relevant practical skills by creating their own individual media production
- apply their knowledge and understanding of media language and representation to express and communicate meaning to an intended audience.

Teacher activities

- Recap the three key areas which are examined in this component, reminding learners that they need to apply their knowledge and understanding of media language and representation in order to communicate meaning to an intended audience.
- Issue and explain the assessment criteria for the component (pages 45–6 of the specification), asking learners to refer to the criteria during the production process, ensuring that they are fulfilling the requirements of the brief.
- Facilitate the production work, ensuring that learners are working in the same form that they will use for their final production.
- Emphasise the importance of the use of original images.

Learner activities

- Learners continue working on their own mini production, ensuring that they are covering the three key areas which are examined in this component: media language; representation; intended audience.
- Learners refer to the assessment criteria, ensuring that they are fulfilling the requirements of the brief.
- Learners ensure that they are using original photography, video footage, graphics, illustrations and artwork as far as possible.

Suggested homework

Learners continue the production work.

Year 1 Week 20b

Introduction to creating media – preliminary production

Learning objectives – learners will be able to:

- use technology to produce a media product
- practise and develop the relevant practical skills by creating their own individual media production
- apply their knowledge and understanding of media language and representation to express and communicate meaning to an intended audience.

Teacher activities

- Recap the three key areas which are examined in this component, reminding learners that they need to apply their knowledge and understanding of media language and representation and how they will target their intended audience.
- Facilitate the production work, reminding learners to use codes and conventions appropriate for the genre and the audience.
- Remind learners to refer to the assessment criteria for the unit and to their Statement of Intent during the production process, ensuring that they are fulfilling the requirements of the brief.

Learner activities

- Learners continue working on their own mini production, ensuring that they are covering the three key areas which are examined in this unit: media language; representation; intended audience.
- Learners refer to the assessment criteria, ensuring that they are fulfilling the requirements of the brief.
- Learners refer to their planning documents and to their Statement of Intent to ensure that they are using appropriate codes and conventions and media language to construct the intended representation for the specified audience.
- Learners ensure that they are using original photography, video footage, graphics, illustrations and artwork as far as possible.

Suggested homework

Learners continue the production work.

Year 1 Week 21a

Introduction to creating media – preliminary production

Learning objectives – learners will be able to:
● use technology to produce a media product
● practise and develop the relevant practical skills by creating their own individual media production
● discuss what has been learned about applying media language and representation to express and communicate meaning to an intended audience
● learn from peers' feedback and from giving feedback to other learners.

Teacher activities

- Emphasise the importance of meeting deadlines, stating that productions must be completed before the next lesson.
- Ask learners to work in pairs, commenting on how far their partner has fulfilled their aims in their Statement of Intent.
- Ask learners to comment on how effectively their partner has used codes and conventions; how well they have used media language to construct stereotypes/anti-stereotypes; how well they have communicated meaning to their target audience.
- Ask learners to make final improvements to their productions based on the feedback received.

Learner activities

- Learners comment on each other's productions, using each other's Statement of Intent and the assessment criteria.
- Learners suggest improvements to each other.
- Learners make final improvements to their productions in preparation for the peer review in the next lesson.

Suggested homework

Learners complete the production work.

Year 1 Week 21b

Introduction to creating media – preliminary production

Learning objectives – learners will be able to:

- discuss and evaluate what has been learned about applying media language and representation to express and communicate meaning to an intended audience
- learn from peers' and teachers' feedback and from giving feedback to other learners.

Teacher activities

- Ask each learner to read out their Statement of Intent before the work is reviewed by their peers.
- Manage peer-group review of the finished productions, asking learners to refer to the assessment criteria and to the individual learner's Statement of Intent in their feedback on one another's work.
- After the review, ask individual learners to write down three points in response to the question 'What went well?' and three points in response to the question 'What do I need to improve on?' in preparation for the final production.
- Direct a plenary discussion on what has been learned about completing productions to a deadline; choosing media language; constructing representations; targeting a specific audience.

Learner activities

- Learners evaluate the relative success of the productions in relation to each learner's Statement of Intent and to the assessment criteria, commenting on: media language; representation; intended audience.
- Learners identify their own strengths and weaknesses in production work, identifying the key areas that need improvement for the final practical production.

Suggested homework

Learners write or record a short self-evaluation of their preliminary production.

Year 1 Week 22a

Creating media – research into existing media products

Learning objectives – learners will be able to:

- understand the detailed requirements of the set briefs
- state the codes and conventions of the media form and/or the specified genre in terms of media language elements, to establish what is conventional and unconventional media language for that media form
- analyse the connotations created by choice of media language in existing products
- analyse how media language creates narrative, portrays aspects of reality, constructs points of view and conveys messages and values.

Key products

The Official Jacqueline Wilson Mag (http://www.jw-mag.com/the-mag/)

The Sarah Jane Adventures (http://www.bbc.co.uk/cbbc/shows/the-sarah-jane-adventures)

One Direction, *What Makes You Beautiful* (https://www.youtube.com/watch?v=QJO3ROT-A4E)

Games for Girls **website** (http://www.girlsgogames.com/)

Teacher activities

- Remind learners of the requirements of the Creating Media component, with its particular focus on media language, representation (including stereotypes and the ways in which representations are constructed) and intended audience.
- Remind learners that they must work individually on this unit, although they can use other learners as models, cast or crew. They must record any assistance from unassessed learners.
- Issue the details of the set briefs, ensuring that the learners understand the full requirements: the length of the product; the genre; the intended audience; the precise instructions on how much found material is permitted; any additional specified details.
- Explain the importance of the 'evidence trail' and that learners must keep a record of their research and planning in a log book or a blog. Reinforce the point that their research findings must inform their planning and final production.
- Display and demonstrate how to analyse and annotate screengrabs from a TV programme or a music video/a front cover of a magazine/a screenshot of a website with a very clear use of media language to construct a particular representation for an intended audience of 10–13 year olds or 14–18 year olds, depending on the brief.

Learner activities

- Learners identify and annotate the following in the exemplar products: uses of codes and conventions and media language; representations; intended audience.
- Learners research existing similar media products in order to plan their own production.
- Learners record this research in a log book or a blog.

Year 1 Week 22b

Creating media – research into intertextuality

Learning objectives – learners will be able to:

- understand the importance of dates and deadlines
- investigate uses of intertextuality in existing products
- analyse the connotations created by choice of media language in existing products
- state how these techniques will or will not be used in the production
- understand how individual research will inform their own practical production.

Key products

Taylor Swift, *Look What You Made Me Do* (https://www.youtube.com/watch?v=3tmd-ClpJxA&list=RD3tmd-ClpJxA)

Madonna, *Material Girl* (https://www.youtube.com/watch?v=6p-lDYPR2P8)

Teacher activities

- Give learners a calendar for the duration of this component, explaining that this will form the basis of their pre-production and production schedule. Give learners interim deadlines. Ask learners to fill in individual deadlines and other commitments.
- Ask learners to look at the indicative content for the relevant brief in the specification. Explain that although intertextuality is not specified in the assessment criteria, it is included in the indicative content for Level 5 for each brief in the SAMs (see pages 48, 50, 52, 54 of the specification). Ask learners to consider the connotations and possible effects of the use of intertextuality, for example: humour, satire, nostalgia, familiarity.
- Ask learners to brainstorm initial ideas for their productions, including possible uses of intertextuality.

Learner activities

- Learners take responsibility for their time management of the production, creating their own individual production schedules with interim deadlines identified by the teacher.
- Learners make notes on intertextuality; research and analyse its uses and connotations in actual media products in the relevant form. They make notes on how they could use intertextuality in their productions.
- Learners continue to identify and analyse key uses of codes and conventions and media language in actual media products.
- Learners brainstorm their initial ideas for their productions, with suggestions for uses of intertextuality.

Suggested homework

Learners continue researching and analysing examples of intertextuality.

Year 1 Week 23a

Creating media – research into stereotyping

Learning objectives – learners will be able to:

- analyse the issues of stereotyping, misrepresentation or under-representation in similar media products
- state how the production aims to construct representations
- state how the production will use anti-stereotyping or include under-represented groups.

Key product

New Statesman, **'Don't worry, Old Etonian Damian Lewis calls claims of privilege in acting "nonsense!"'** (http://www.newstatesman.com/culture/film/2017/02/don-t-worry-old-etonian-damian-lewis-says-worries-over-lack-working-class)

Teacher activities

- Ask learners to write three statements identifying stereotypes and anti-stereotypes concerning class.
- Ask learners to read the *New Statesman* article.
- Ask learners to research, analyse and record examples of anti-stereotypes in their logs, such as the successful black British working-class actor/writer/director Noel Clarke.
- Explain the terms misrepresentation and under-representation (e.g. older women or disabled presenters on television). Looking at the indicative content for the relevant brief in the specification (pages 48, 50, 52, 54), explain to learners that anti-stereotyping and/or the representation of a misrepresented or under-represented group is expected in their productions in order to achieve Level 5.
- Ask learners to state in their logs how they will construct representations and whether they will use stereotypes, anti-stereotypes, misrepresented or under-represented groups in their productions.

Learner activities

- Learners consider stereotypes and anti-stereotypes in relation to class, using the *New Statesman* article as a starting point.
- Learners research, analyse and record further examples of anti-stereotypes, analysing how effectively they convey messages and values.
- Learners state in their logs how they intend to construct representations in their productions and whether they intend to use stereotypes, anti-stereotypes, misrepresented or under-represented groups in their productions.

Suggested homework

Learners continue researching examples of anti-stereotypes, misrepresentations and under-represented groups.

Year 1 Week 23b

Creating media – research into narrative

Learning objectives – learners will be able to:

- analyse how media language creates narrative, portrays aspects of reality, constructs points of view, and conveys messages and values
- analyse the issues of stereotyping, misrepresentation or under-representation in similar media products
- state how the production aims to construct representations
- state how the production will use anti-stereotyping or include under-represented groups.

Key product

Daily Telegraph, **'Ed Sheeran: the stories behind his best songs'** (http://www.telegraph.co.uk/music/what-to-listen-to/stories-behind-ed-sheerans-best-songs/5/)

Teacher activities

- Explain the importance of narrative in the learners' productions, particularly if narrative structure is listed in the minimum requirements for the brief.
- Ensure that learners understand and can use the following terms: opening, equilibrium, enigma, quest, causality, tension, suspense, closure/resolution.
- Explain that elements of narrative structure can be identified even in magazine articles and websites, using Propp's theory of the 'magic agent' and Propp's character roles or functions: hero, villain, false hero, princess, donor, helper, dispatcher (https://www.bbc.co.uk/education/guides/zgydhv4/revision). This could be exemplified by directing learners to a specific magazine article such as the *Daily Telegraph* article.
- Ask learners to use Propp's narrative theory to analyse actual media products.
- Ask learners to consider narrative structure and character roles in their own production, identifying how these narrative elements will contribute to representation.

Learner activities

- Learners identify, analyse and record narrative structure in actual media products.
- Learners consider how the elements of narrative structure, particularly character roles and functions, contribute to representation (including stereotypes and anti-stereotypes).
- Learners state how they will use narrative elements to contribute to representation in their own productions.

Suggested homework

Learners continue researching narrative elements, stereotypes and anti-stereotypes.

Year 1 Week 24a

Creating media – research into target audiences

> ### Learning objectives – learners will be able to:
>
> - discuss the style of media language that is commonly used for the target audience
> - outline what may serve to alienate or patronise the target audience and what may make them feel included or flattered
> - identify and research their target audience
> - state how the production aims to address the target audience.

Key product

BBC Bitesize (http://www.bbc.co.uk/education/guides/zy24p39/revision)

Teacher activities

- Ask learners to research audiences using BBC Bitesize.
- Ask learners to consider the use of demographics, psychographics, lifestyle, interests and other media products likely to be consumed by their audience to help build their audience profile.
- Ask learners to build a profile of their target audience in their logs by producing a mood board for a typical audience member.
- Explain the term mode of address and ask learners to carry out a detailed analysis of the mode of address of a relevant media product. How specifically does the product address and aim to include its audience? Is there anything patronising or alienating in the language used? Is intertextuality used?

Learner activities

- Learners design a mood board for a typical audience member for their production, using psychographics, lifestyle, interests and other media products likely to be consumed by their audience.
- Learners carry out a detailed analysis of the mode of address of a magazine/television programme/music video/website, analysing how the product addresses and aims to include its audience.
- Learners write a brief statement on how they intend to address and include their target audience and whether they intend to include intertextual references.

Suggested homework

Learners finish their detailed analysis of the mode of address of a relevant media product.

Year 1 Week 24b

Creating media – planning: Statement of Intent

Learning objectives – learners will be able to:

- draft the Statement of Intent
- state how media language will be used to communicate meaning
- state how representations will be identified and used
- state how the target audience will be identified, reached and addressed
- state how they have interpreted and responded to research findings.

Teacher activities

- Explain the importance of the Statement of Intent, emphasising that it is a compulsory element and that learners can reach only a maximum number of 18 marks (the top of Level 3) if they fail to provide the statement.
- Emphasise the importance of keeping to the word length (250–300 words).
- Explain to learners that they will have a chance to redraft and add to their statement after they have pitched their production to the class in a few weeks' time.
- Give learners the details that must be included in the statement:

  1. details of the brief
  2. how they intend to use media language to communicate meaning through their selection of forms, codes and conventions
  3. how they identify and use specific representations of events, issues, individuals or social groups (including the use of stereotypes and anti-stereotypes)
  4. how they intend to identify, reach and address their target audience (including the use of intertextuality)
  5. how they have interpreted and responded to their research findings during the planning and production process.

Learner activities

- Learners draft the Statement of Intent.
- Learners begin planning the finer details of their production, recording them in their logs.

Suggested homework

Learners continue planning their productions.

Year 1 Week 25a

Creating media – planning checklist

> ## Learning objectives – learners will be able to:
> - outline the time-line for the production
> - state the resources needed for the production, including use of crew
> - state how the target audience will be identified, reached and addressed
> - state how they have interpreted and responded to research findings.

Teacher activities

- Give learners the date (allowing approximately three weeks) for their pitches to be presented to the rest of the class.
- Give learners a planning checklist outlining the relevant areas they should aim to complete by that date:

  1. locations/sets
  2. casting of models/actors
  3. supporting crew members and their roles
  4. props/costumes
  5. shooting/production schedule
  6. storyboard/mock-ups/test shots
  7. script/first draft of written copy for a magazine double-page spread/first draft of written copy for website article/first draft of designs for front cover or website
  8. equipment needed
  9. the results of audience research
  10. risk assessment.

Learner activities

- Learners plan the details of their production, recording these in their logs.
- Learners ensure that they carry out a recce of their intended locations and make any necessary arrangements to use them.
- Learners ask any unassessed learners to support them as crew, actors or models, keeping a detailed record of requests and responses.

Suggested homework

Learners continue planning their productions.

Year 1 Week 25b

Creating media – planning and pre-production

Learning objectives – learners will be able to:

- state the resources needed for the production, including use of crew
- produce a draft/storyboard/mock-up for the production
- demonstrate in their drafts/storyboards/mock-ups how media language will be used to communicate meaning to their intended audience
- demonstrate in their drafts/storyboard/mock-ups how representations will be identified and used.

Teacher activities

- Check that each learner has filled in their production schedule calendar, giving advice on the time needed for each stage of the production.
- Check learners' locations and risk assessments, giving advice for improvements on any health and safety issues.
- Check learners' list of required technical resources (availability, pre-booking, etc.).
- Remind learners of the planning areas which need to be completed by the pitch date. Ask them to select five of the planning areas from the checklist below (including a shooting schedule and a first draft or script) and aim to complete them by the end of the week:

  1. locations/sets
  2. casting of models/actors
  3. supporting crew members and their roles
  4. props/costumes
  5. shooting/production schedule
  6. storyboard/mock-ups/test shots
  7. script/first draft of written copy for a magazine double-page spread/first draft of written copy for website article
  8. equipment needed
  9. the results of audience research
  10. risk assessment.

Learner activities

- Learners record their planning in their logs.
- Learners write down the details of any planned shoots/recordings and compile them into a call list which they give to any unassessed learners, models or actors.
- Learners adjust production schedules, locations and risk assessments following the advice of the teacher.

Suggested homework

Learners continue recording their planning, writing their first drafts or scripts and planning layouts and storyboards.

Year 1 Week 26a

Creating media – planning and audience research

Learning objectives – learners will be able to:

- research what may serve to alienate or patronise the target audience and what may make them feel included or flattered
- reflect on how media language will be used to communicate meaning
- reflect on how representations will be identified and used
- state how the target audience will be identified, reached and addressed
- state how they have interpreted and responded to research findings.

Teacher activities

- Check learners' progress in planning.
- Support learners in trouble-shooting any problems that have arisen.
- Ask learners to produce questionnaires for an audience survey in order to test out their plans on their target audience.
- Ask learners to conduct two in-depth interviews with potential members of their target audience. These could be recorded on their mobiles or using school/college equipment.
- Suggest the following as some of the key points learners could include in their audience research:

  1. Is the title of their magazine/TV programme/website appropriate?

  2. Is the mode of address inclusive/patronising/appropriate?

  3. Is the use of media language conventional or does it break conventions, and does this seem appropriate for the target audience?

  4. Do the models/actors/images appeal to the target audience?

  5. How does the target audience respond to the planned representation/use of stereotypes/anti-stereotypes?

  6. How well does the target audience understand the intended messages and values?

Learner activities

- Learners produce questionnaires for a quantitative audience survey on their planned production.
- Learners produce four in-depth questions for two individual interviews with potential members of their target audience.
- Learners conduct and record two individual in-depth interviews with potential members of their target audience.
- Learners evaluate their research findings.

Suggested homework

Learners continue to reflect on and evaluate their audience research findings and make any adjustments necessary to their planned productions.

Year 1 Week 26b

Creating media – planning and original material

Learning objectives – learners will be able to:

- state how they have interpreted and responded to research findings
- understand the requirements for original footage, images and text
- state how media language will be used to communicate meaning
- state how representations will be identified and used.

Teacher activities

- Check that learners have reflected on and evaluated their audience research findings and responded to them by making changes where appropriate to their production plans and to their Statement of Intent.

- Ask learners to look at the instructions for Creating Media on page 43 of the specification, reminding them that if they overuse found footage, images or text, they will be limited to 18 marks out of 30 (the top of Level 3).

- Ask learners to look again at the minimum requirements of the relevant set brief and to check that they are including enough original material. For example, the SAM magazine brief requires five original images, with an original masthead/title, original main cover image and at least two other original images on the front cover and at least two other original images in the double-page spread article.

- Ask learners to work in pairs to check that their partner has covered the requirements for original footage, images and text in their planning material.

- Ask learners to check that their partner has covered the other detailed requirements of the brief in their planning material.

Learner activities

- Learners adapt their planning in response to audience research and adjust the section on target audience in their Statement of Intent where necessary.

- In pairs, learners check their partner's planning material to see that their productions will fulfil the requirements for original footage, images and text, and that the productions will fulfil the other detailed requirements of the brief.

- Learners use a planning checklist to ensure that they have covered all areas of pre-production.

Suggested homework

Learners continue planning and finalising the details of the production and the production schedule.

Year 1 Week 27a

Creating media – planning the pitch

Learning objectives – learners will be able to:

- prepare a pitch for their production to be presented to the rest of the class
- state the details of how and when they intend to use crew/models/actors
- state how media language will be used to communicate meaning
- state how representations will be constructed
- state how they intend to reach their target audience
- check their planning against their Statement of Intent.

Teacher activities

- Ask learners to plan their pitches (to last no more than two minutes) to present to the rest of the class, and to be prepared to answer questions.
- Explain to learners that they must include the following:

  1. a brief summary of the content of their production

  2. the representations they intend to construct, including the use of anti-stereotypes

  3. two examples of how they aim to appeal to their target audience through the use of an image/ title/mode of address/sequence of images/intertextuality, fitting in with their audience research

  4. the names of any models/actors/supporting crew members

  5. selected locations/sets

  6. planned dates for photoshoots/filming.

Learner activities

- Learners prepare their pitches, dealing with any problem areas and ensuring that they are prepared to answer questions.
- Learners check that their pitches match their Statement of Intent.

Suggested homework

Learners continue preparing pitches and finalising their planning.

Year 1 Week 27b

Creating media – presenting the pitch

Learning objectives – learners will be able to:

- present a pitch for their production to the rest of the class
- answer questions on their production from the rest of the class
- outline the time-line for the production
- state the resources needed for the production, including use of crew
- state how media language will be used to communicate meaning
- state how representations will be identified and used
- state how the target audience will be identified, reached and addressed
- state how they have interpreted and responded to research findings.

Teacher activities

- Organise the presentation of the pitches and the question and answer sessions.
- Ask learners to reflect on the responses to their pitch and adapt scripts, titles, layouts and modes of address if necessary.
- Check that the planning material is up to date and identify any missing areas.

Learner activities

- Learners listen to one another's pitches.
- Learners give feedback on/ask questions about one another's productions.
- Learners adapt or discard any elements of their production which have been identified as problematic.
- Learners check how closely their planning fits their Statement of Intent, adapting it if necessary.

Suggested homework

Learners record responses to their pitch and any adaptations they have made. Learners finalise the details of the production and the production schedule.

Year 1 Weeks 28–29

Creating media – production phase 1

This material covers four hours.

Learning objectives – learners will be able to:

- use technology to produce a media product
- manage the resources needed for the production, including use of crew
- use storyboards/mock-ups/drafts to produce a media product
- direct actors/models/crew in order to achieve the planned representation/s for an intended audience
- use media language to construct the planned representation/s for an intended audience
- use their risk assessments during production.

Teacher activities

- Organise and issue the necessary equipment, supporting learners where necessary; for example, with the use of lighting, green-screen, Photoshop, use of website templates.
- Remind learners to keep checking their progress against their plans and their Statement of Intent.
- Facilitate the production work, particularly with regard to unassessed learners.
- Remind learners to record the use of sources and log the use of unassessed learners.
- Work with individual learners on problems over locations, health and safety, equipment, unassessed learners.
- Remind learners that if any found material is used, it must be kept to a minimum and the sources must be clearly identified and acknowledged.

Learner activities

- Learners work on production, with close reference to their storyboards/mock-ups/drafts.
- Learners manage crew if necessary, recording the work of any unassessed learners.
- Learners organise sets, locations, lighting, props, costumes and mise-en-scène before shooting original footage or still images.
- Learners direct models/actors on shoots.
- Learners use a variety of shots.
- Learners check that interim deadlines and production dates are manageable, altering them if necessary.

Suggested homework

Learners continue working on their productions, matching them against the intended audience and their Statement of Intent.

Year 1 Week 30

Creating media – production phase 1 (focus on editing)

This material covers two hours.

Learning objectives – learners will be able to:

- use technology to produce a media product
- edit original material to express and communicate meaning to the intended audience
- edit original material in order to construct specific representations as outlined in the Statement of Intent
- use the indicative content from the specification to inform the production of a media product
- use media language to construct the planned representation/s for an intended audience.

Teacher activities

- Remind learners of interim deadline 1 in the following week: 40 seconds of their TV programme or music video must be edited; the first page of their magazine or website must be complete.
- Facilitate the editing work, supporting learners with technical issues.
- Using the indicative content for the relevant brief, give learners a checklist with detailed points such as the ones below to help them keep their intended audience in mind.

    - **Magazines** – appropriate typography with a consistent house style, creating a brand identity; appropriate layout; appropriate use of language, tone, mode of address; images integrated with text; a clear attempt to construct a particular representation.
    - **Television** – appropriate and clear narrative; appropriate use of mise-en-scène; a variety of shots appropriate to the genre; appropriate pace of editing; a clear attempt to construct a particular representation.
    - **Music video** – appropriate, clear narrative; appropriate use of mise-en-scène; a variety of shots appropriate to the music genre; appropriate use of editing devices for the genre; a clear attempt to construct a particular representation.
    - **Website** – appropriate typography with a consistent house style, creating a brand identity; appropriate layout and page design with menu, navigation bar, links; appropriate use of language, tone, mode of address; embedded audio or video; opportunities for audience interactivity; integrated images with text; a clear attempt to construct a particular representation.

Learner activities

- Learners edit their original material, with close reference to the checklists from the indicative content to ensure that they will meet the requirements of the brief.

Suggested homework

Learners continue working on their productions.

Year 1 Week 31

Creating media – production: interim deadline 1

This material covers two hours.

> ### Learning objectives – learners will be able to:
>
> - use technology to produce a media product
> - evaluate the success of the first phase of the production
> - learn from peers' feedback and from giving feedback to other learners
> - write an action plan for changes needed.

Teacher activities

- Ask learners to work in pairs, using their partner's Statement of Intent and the checklist from the indicative content (see Week 30) to review each other's work.
- Ask learners to comment on how far their partner has fulfilled their aims and the requirements of the brief.
- Ask individual learners to write an action plan for any changes needed, such as reshoots, and to review their production schedules and deadlines.

Learner activities

- In pairs, learners review and comment on each other's productions, using each other's Statement of Intent and the checklist from the indicative content (see Week 30).
- Learners evaluate their individual progress, writing a brief action plan for necessary changes or improvements, such as reshoots.
- Learners review their production schedule if necessary.

Suggested homework

Learners continue into the second phase of their productions.

Year 1 Weeks 32–34

Creating media – production phase 2

This material covers four hours.

Learning objectives – learners will be able to:

- use technology to produce a media product
- use media language to construct the planned representation/s for an intended audience
- edit original material to express and communicate meaning to the intended audience
- edit original material in order to construct specific representations as outlined in the Statement of Intent
- use the indicative content from the specification to inform the production of a media product.

Teacher activities

- Remind learners of interim deadline 2 in two to three weeks' time: 80 seconds of their TV programme or music video must be edited; the first two pages of their magazine or website must be complete.
- Facilitate the editing work, supporting learners with technical issues.
- Remind learners to keep checking their progress against their plans, their Statement of Intent and the relevant checklist from the indicative content.
- Remind learners of the importance of demonstrating their knowledge of representation and of the relevant codes and conventions.

Learner activities

- Learners continue to work on production and editing, with close reference to their storyboards/mock-ups/drafts and the relevant checklist from the indicative content.
- Learners continue to manage crew and direct models/actors, remembering to record the work of any unassessed learners.
- Learners continue to organise sets, locations, lighting, props, costumes and mise-en-scène before shooting original footage or still images.
- Learners check production and post-production dates in order to meet interim deadline 2, altering them if necessary.

Suggested homework

Learners continue working on their productions.

Year 1 Week 35

Creating media – production: interim deadline 2

This material covers two hours.

> ## Learning objectives – learners will be able to:
> - use technology to produce a media product
> - evaluate the success of the second phase of the production
> - learn from peers' feedback and from giving feedback to other learners
> - write an action plan for changes needed.

Teacher activities

- Ask learners to work in groups, commenting on the relative success of the first two phases of production, using the checklist below from the indicative content to review one another's progress:

  1. **Magazines** – appropriate typography with some variation within a consistent house style; appropriate layout and page design with graphics; appropriate use of language, tone, mode of address; appropriate use of mise-en-scène; brand identity; a clear attempt to construct a particular representation, as outlined in the Statement of Intent.

  2. **Television** – appropriate and clear narrative; appropriate use of mise-en-scène; a variety of shots appropriate to the genre; appropriate pace of continuity editing; use of appropriate soundtrack; a clear attempt to construct a particular representation, as outlined in the Statement of Intent.

  3. **Music video** – appropriate and clear narrative; appropriate use of mise-en-scène; a variety of shots appropriate to the genre of music; appropriate pace and use of editing devices for the genre of music; a clear attempt to construct a particular representation.

  4. **Website** – appropriate typography with a consistent house style; appropriate layout and page design with menu, navigation bar, links, logos, graphics; appropriate use of language, tone, mode of address; brand identity; embedded audio or video; opportunities for audience interactivity and user-generated content; a clear attempt to construct a particular representation.

Learner activities

- In groups, learners review and comment on one another's productions, using the checklist from the indicative content.
- Learners evaluate their individual progress, writing a brief action plan for necessary changes or improvements.
- Learners make any final changes to their production schedule if necessary.

Suggested homework

Learners continue into the third and final phase of their productions.

Year 1 Weeks 36–38

Creating media – production phase 3

This material covers four hours.

Learning objectives – learners will be able to:

- use technology to produce a media product
- use media language to construct the planned representation/s for an intended audience
- edit original material to express and communicate meaning to the intended audience
- edit original material in order to construct specific representations as outlined in the Statement of Intent
- use the indicative content from the specification to inform the production of a media product.

Teacher activities

- Remind learners of their final deadline in two to three weeks' time: their TV programme or music video must be edited and complete, lasting approximately two minutes; the three pages of their magazine must be complete; the two pages of the website must be complete, including 45 seconds of embedded audio-visual or audio material.
- Facilitate the editing work, supporting learners with technical issues.
- Remind learners to keep checking their progress against their plans, their Statement of Intent and the relevant checklist from the indicative content.

Learner activities

- Learners continue to work on production and editing, with close reference to their storyboards/mock-ups/drafts and the relevant checklist from the indicative content.
- Learners continue to manage crew and direct models/actors, remembering to record the work of any unassessed learners.
- Learners continue to organise sets, locations, lighting, props, costumes and mise-en-scène before shooting original footage or still images.
- Learners check production and post-production dates in order to meet the final deadline, altering them if necessary.

Suggested homework

Learners continue working on their productions.

Year 1 Week 39a

Creating media – final deadline and peer-group review

> ### Learning objectives – learners will be able to:
>
> - use technology to produce a media product
> - discuss and evaluate what has been learned about applying media language and representation to express and communicate meaning to an intended audience
> - learn from and act on peers' feedback and from giving feedback to other learners
> - action plan any further work needed on the production before the final submission.

Teacher activities

- Screen or display each learner's production in turn, asking others to comment on how effectively the learner has used media language; how well they have constructed representation/s; how effectively they have targeted their intended audience, using the assessment criteria. It may be useful to display the relevant indicative content from the SAMs here in order to ensure attention to detail.
- Ask the learner whose work is being reviewed how closely their production matches their Statement of Intent.
- Manage the peer review, asking learners to make suggestions for any final small improvements: cuts/deletions/additions/adaptations.
- Action plan any further work that needs completion (under teacher supervision in additional catch-up sessions).
- Ask learners to make small final improvements to their productions based on the feedback received.

Learner activities

- Using the assessment criteria and the indicative content, other learners comment on how effectively the learner whose work is being reviewed has used media language; constructed representations; targeted the intended audience.
- Learners suggest small improvements: cuts/deletions/additions/adaptations.
- Learners make final improvements to their productions.

Suggested homework

Learners complete the production work, making any necessary final improvements.

Year 1 Week 39b

Creating media – final submission

Learning objectives – learners will be able to:

- discuss and evaluate what has been learned about applying media language and representation to express and communicate meaning to an intended audience
- reflect on how they have interpreted and responded to research findings during the planning and production process
- learn from and act on peers' feedback and from giving feedback to other learners.

Teacher activities

- Complete the peer-group review of learners' productions.
- Encourage learners to make final small improvements based on the feedback received in order to improve their use of media language; the representation/s constructed; how far the production targets its intended audience.
- Action plan any further work that needs completion (under teacher supervision in additional catch-up sessions).
- Ask learners to complete cover sheets, ensuring that they reference all sources used in the production and all uses of unassessed learners.

Learner activities

- Learners finish commenting on one another's productions, focusing on the use of media language, the construction of representation and how effectively the target audience is addressed, using the assessment criteria.
- Learners make any necessary improvements based on the peer group feedback: cuts/deletions/additions/adaptations to their productions.
- Learners complete the cover sheets, ensuring that they reference all sources used in the production and all uses of unassessed learners.

Year 2 Week 1a

Introduction to media industries

> ### Learning objectives – learners will be able to:
> - define the terms 'media conglomerate', 'vertical integration', 'diversification', 'convergence'
> - exemplify the above terms using Warner Bros and *The Lego Movie/The Lego Movie* video game as a case study.

Key product

Box Office Mojo website (http://www.boxofficemojo.com/)

Teacher activities

- Remind learners that *The Lego Movie* and *The Lego Movie* video game are the set products for Promoting Media.
- Display a range of American film studios' logos. Have direct discussion of prior knowledge.
- Provide learners with a list of terms ('media conglomerate', 'vertical integration', 'diversification', 'convergence'). Ensure that full, accurate definitions are provided.
- Arrange access to computers.
- Facilitate a working list of Time Warner's main competitors as learners conduct research.
- Prepare for the homework task by introducing the Box Office Mojo website, perhaps explaining key terms such as 'box office' and 'gross'.

Learner activities

- Learners individually write down which studios they know of/recognise and then find out whether any films they know of were produced by those studios.
- In pairs, learners try to record a definition against each term, then compare their own understanding with the correct definition provided by the teacher.
- Using computers, learners establish key information about Time Warner and its operating divisions. Ensure that they understand that Warner Bros is a division of Time Warner.
- Learners submit their findings on key competitors as they investigate further.

Suggested homework

Learners research box office takings by studio on the Box Office Mojo website to compare Warner Bros with the other American studios. They could select three Warner Bros films and two other studios. They then order the films in terms of box office success and suggest reasons.

Year 2 Week 1b

Introduction to media industries

Learning objectives – learners will be able to:

- define the terms 'media conglomerate', 'vertical integration', 'diversification', 'convergence'
- explain the role of the BBFC in regulating film in the UK.

Key products

The Lego Movie film
The Lego Movie video game

Teacher activities

- Provide sets of cards, one set with the following terms on them and the other with their definitions: 'media conglomerate', 'vertical integration', 'diversification', 'convergence'.
- Introduce new key terminology – blockbuster, marketing and synergy – in relation to *The Lego Movie* and *The Lego Movie* video game.
- Facilitate small- and whole-group discussion, encouraging the use of correct terminology.
- Introduce the need for regulation in industry and the specific role of the British Board of Film Classification (BBFC).

Learner activities

- In pairs, learners match definitions with the correct terms.
- In small groups, learners discuss and agree reasons why Time Warner has diversified into video games and how this is an example of vertical integration, using *The Lego Movie* as a case study. They should focus on the financial and promotional benefits of releasing films alongside other products. Learners feed back to the class, ensuring that all the terminology is used in their presentation.
- Individually, learners compile a list of hypothetical consequences/outcomes of an unregulated film industry.

Suggested homework

Using http://www.bbfc.co.uk as the source of information, learners prepare a five- to ten-slide presentation about film regulation in the UK.

Year 2 Week 2a

Introduction to media industries

> ### Learning objectives – learners will be able to:
>
> - Explain the influence of the cultural supremacy of comic book franchises in Hollywood on Hollywood film production.

Key products

The Lego Movie poster campaign:

1. The main poster featuring an ensemble cast, running from danger (http://www.impawards. com/2014/lego_movie_ver9.html)

2. Character poster of Vitruvius in close-up (http://www.impawards.com/2014/lego_movie_ver3. html)

3. Character poster of Emmet in close-up (http://www.impawards.com/2014/lego_movie_ver8. html)

4. Character poster of Lord Business in close-up (http://www.impawards.com/2014/lego_movie_ ver5.html)

5. Character poster of Wyldstyle in close-up (http://www.impawards.com/2014/lego_movie_ver7. html)

Teacher activities

- Provide learners with a classic Marvel comic book image of Spider-Man and display *The Lego Movie* poster of Emmet.

- Explain the influence of the cultural supremacy of comic book franchises in Hollywood on Hollywood film production. Lead discussion of learners' prior knowledge of comic books that have given rise to Hollywood blockbusters.

- Provide learners with brief examples of classic comic book characters (e.g. Wonder Woman) and ask them to record (filling in a table) how placing that character in different social, political, cultural and historical contexts can affect their representation and how audiences receive them.

- Provide key dates and events in twentieth-century America/Britain to aid learners.

Learner activities

- Learners review previous analysis of media language and representations in the posters through a labelled comparison of Emmet (character poster in close-up) with Spider-Man. They focus on the differences in representation, ensuring use of media language in the written labels.

- In pairs, learners take a comic book character and move him or her through the early twentieth century, considering how the character might be viewed or represented.

Suggested homework

Look up the definition of a blockbuster on Wikipedia. Then research franchises on the Box Office Mojo website (http://www.boxofficemojo.com/). Which companies are involved in the production of *Toy Story*?

Year 2 Week 2b

Introduction to media industries

Learning objectives – learners will be able to:

- explain the influence of commercially and critically successful multi-layered films aimed at children and adults (e.g. *Toy Story*) on Hollywood film production

- explain the influence of 'popular feminism' within a patriarchal industry on women's roles in action films

- explain how the media language and representations in the advertising target a mass audience

- explore different possible audience interpretations of the advertising campaign (e.g. enthusiastic, unengaged, oppositional) and possible reasons for these.

Key products

The Lego Movie posters:

1. The main poster featuring an ensemble cast, running from danger (http://www.impawards. com/2014/lego_movie_ver9.html)

2. Character poster of Wyldstyle in close-up (http://www.impawards.com/2014/lego_ movie_ver7.html)

Toy Story (1995) Disney Pixar

Teacher activities

- Display some of the merchandise connected with *Toy Story*. Facilitate discussion surrounding the definition and benefits of franchising.

- Show an extract from *Toy Story* and ask learners to reflect on key themes such as alienation and abandonment. Introduce the notion of multi-layered narrative. Perhaps distribute some positive reviews and box office statistics.

- Focus on Wyldstyle as an action heroine. Explain the influence of 'popular feminism' within a patriarchal industry on women's roles in action films. Perhaps provide images of a range of other action heroines. Encourage links to adult themes.

- Facilitate discussion of any potential alternative audience interpretations of the ensemble cast poster.

Learner activities

- Individually, learners compile a list of three benefits provided to Hollywood by the use of franchising.

- Learners identify adult themes within *Toy Story* and discuss why these may be accessible and relevant to children too.

- In groups, learners compile a list of action heroines, their main representations as characters and the mainstream pleasures provided by their characters (e.g. easily identifiable, comedy and spectacle). Compare and contrast the codes and conventions used to target mass audiences in the different films learners list.

- Individually, learners write a 15-minute essay on how Wyldstyle demonstrates social and cultural relevance to mass audiences.

- As a group, learners discuss possible audience interpretations of the advertising campaign.

Suggested homework

Learners compare the representation of Wyldstyle with another female action heroine from the advertising for a film of their choice.

Year 2 Week 3a

Promoting media – film

Learning objectives – learners will be able to:

- outline how the media language and representations in the TV trailer target a mass family audience
- explain the funding of Hollywood studios, including the role of merchandising
- explain the role of marketing in Hollywood blockbusters
- explain the synergy that led to other companies producing television advertising that also advertised *The Lego Movie*.

Key product

The Lego Movie ITV ad break (February 2014) (https://www.youtube.com/watch?v=HSbYBzUEQlc)

Teacher activities

- Facilitate a brief class discussion about what family means to students. Perhaps display an image of a range of families.
- Explain the funding of Hollywood studios and highlight the role of merchandising.
- Screen *The Lego Movie* advert break originally aired during *Dancing on Ice* (ITV, 6.15pm).
- Facilitate a discussion explaining the synergy that led to other companies producing television advertising that also advertised *The Lego Movie*.
- Arrange for access to computers.

Learner activities

- In pairs, learners establish a list of films that appeal to a mass family audience. Alongside each film, learners provide four reasons that make that film appealing to a family.
- As a class, learners discuss the appeal of family audiences to Hollywood studios, focusing on how the studios can maximise revenues through box office sales in addition to TV sales, product placement, merchandising, DVD sales, etc.
- As a class, learners discuss the marketing value and power for the companies involved in collaborating with a prestige product to make a Lego version of their advert.
- Learners begin to research film marketing in the six weeks leading to release.

Suggested homework

Learners research the marketing for one recent Hollywood blockbuster film.

Year 2 Week 3b

Promoting media – film

Learning objectives – learners will be able to:

- outline how the media language and representations in the TV trailer target a mass family audience
- explain the funding of Hollywood studios, including the role of merchandising
- explain the role of marketing in Hollywood blockbusters.

Key products

The Lego Movie **UK TV trailer and ad break** (https://www.youtube.com/watch?v=HSbYBzUEQlc)

The Lego Movie poster **campaign,** as per Week 2a

Teacher activities

- Screen *The Lego Movie* trailer (which comes after the ad break in the YouTube clip). Provide learners with a blank table to annotate.
- Screen *The Lego Movie* ITV advert break. Ask learners to focus on how the media language targets a mass family audience.
- Arrange access to computers.
- Facilitate learners' presentations. Perhaps collate and copy these for future reference in the case study.
- Encourage learners to discuss their homework findings and analyse the results against *The Lego Movie* marketing campaign.

Learner activities

- Learners view the trailer and advert break, making notes on media representations of events, issues, individuals and social groups.
- In pairs, learners focus on how media language is targeting a mass family audience in its marketing materials. They produce a five-slide presentation, selecting key still images to exemplify their findings.
- Individually, learners establish how the film they researched for homework compares to or differs from *The Lego Movie* marketing campaign.
- Learners research the function of regulation in advertising.

Suggested homework

Learners compile a folder for *The Lego Movie* case study, ensuring that all work and notes are collated for future reference.

Year 2 Week 4a

Promoting media – video games

Learning objectives – learners will be able to:

- explain the uses and gratifications offered by video games
- state the role of technology in audience consumption of video games.

Key products

A range of video games

The Lego Movie **video game walkthroughs** (http://uk.ign.com/wikis/the-lego-movie-video-game/Walkthrough)

Additional resources

Historical consoles: http://www.bbc.co.uk/news/technology-38595543

Current consoles: http://www.bbc.co.uk/newsround/14633761

Uses and gratifications: https://www.bbc.co.uk/education/guides/zg24frd/revision/3

UK gaming statistics: https://www.statista.com/topics/1763/gaming-in-the-united-kingdom/

Teacher activities

- Display images of a range of current video games platforms: consoles, popular mobile apps, PCs, etc.
- Display images of some historic consoles. Then display the two slides together. Emphasise the role of technology in how audiences consume video games.
- Provide learners with a series of flash cards (perhaps with definitions) stating the 'needs': diversion, personal relationships, personal identity, surveillance. Explain the uses and gratifications theory in detail.
- Introduce then facilitate an in-class survey to examine the group's consumption of video games. Highlight audience consumption and compile a log of the class's knowledge of video gaming and the industry.
- Provide learners with some key statistics on gaming in the UK.

Learner activities

- As a class, learners discuss prior knowledge of video games. Using the visual stimulus, learners consider the ways in which video games have developed over time and link these changes to advances in technology.
- Individually, learners take notes on uses and gratifications theory.
- Learners write a mini-essay about their own relationship with video games, speculating about uses and gratifications they (or others, if they are not gamers) derive from their experience of gaming.
- Learners create, and then conduct, a short survey of classmates to establish how widespread gaming is among their peers.
- In pairs, learners speculate about key statistics on the global gaming market, for example the number of gamers, how profitable the industry is, sales figures for specific games.

Suggested homework

Learners watch some of another walkthrough for *The Lego Movie* video game. They write down three ways this game offers uses and gratifications to its player.

Year 2 Week 4b

Promoting media – video games

> ### Learning objectives – learners will be able to:
> - state how games companies market games to target audiences
> - identify the role of the Games Rating Authority in regulating video games
> - state how PEGI ratings categorise audiences.

Key products

A range of appropriate video games

The Games Rating Authority website (http://gamesratingauthority.org/Home/)

Teacher activities

- Provide learners with the front covers of a range of obviously contrasting video games alongside *The Lego Movie* video game.
- Facilitate discussion of the profile of a classic *Lego Movie* gamer, focusing analysis on gender and age.
- Divide the class into mixed-gender groups and allocate the front covers at random.
- Challenge groups to consider how genre might influence audience by displaying a range on the board (perhaps first-person shooter, sports, match 3, family simulations).
- Display the Games Rating Authority website. Explore the purpose and role of the organisation.

Learner activities

- In pairs, learners consider the ways in which the games companies have targeted their audiences.
- In groups, learners devise the profile of the key target audience for the game they have been allocated. They consider any other potential audience types the game could capture.
- Groups feed back their findings to the class.
- As a class, learners discuss the impact of genre on audience.
- Learners take notes on the purpose and role of the Games Rating Authority.
- In pairs, learners consider why such a body is necessary.

Suggested homework

Learners visit the Games Rating Authority website and create a document that outlines the categories of audience defined by the PEGI rating system, including acceptable content for each rating.

Year 2 Week 5a

Promoting media – video games and film

Learning objectives – learners will be able to:

- explain how *The Lego Movie* video game offers uses and gratifications to its audience
- explain how *The Lego Movie* video game uses intertextuality to promote the film.

Key product

***The Lego Movie* video game walkthrough:** Level 2 Escape from Bricksburg (http://uk.ign.com/wikis/the-lego-movie-video-game/Level_2_-_Escape_From_Bricksburg)

Teacher activities

- Explain the uses and gratifications theory to ensure understanding.
- Screen the walkthrough, perhaps focusing on the use of Pac-Man.
- Facilitate discussion of how the video game utilises this intertextuality to help promote the film.
- Screen extracts from other walkthroughs.

Learner activities

- Individually, learners take notes on the uses and gratifications theory.
- In pairs, learners identify uses and gratifications offered to different members of *The Lego Movie*'s gaming audience.
- In small groups, learners identify examples of intertextuality in the walkthrough(s) they have studied.
- In small groups, learners consider the intertextual choices made by the video game producers and explain why a specific intertextual reference might be beneficial for marketing and promotional purposes.
- In small groups, learners discuss how use of a historic game such as Pac-Man may also be relevant to a family audience spanning two generations.

Suggested homework

Learners write the following essay: 'Explain how video games offer uses and gratifications, using *The Lego Movie* video game as an example.'

Year 2 Week 5b

Promoting media – video games and film

> ### Learning objectives – learners will be able to:
> - discuss how audiences might interpret *The Lego Movie* video game differently and why this might be so (e.g. gender, age)
> - explain the influence of the social context that audiences now accept and expect merchandising for major films
> - state that Time Warner is a global media conglomerate funded commercially, owned by shareholders, that uses film as a prestige product to sell convergent products.

Key product

The Lego Movie **video game walkthrough:** Level 7 Attack on Cloud Cuckoo Land (http://uk.ign.com/wikis/the-lego-movie-video-game/Walkthrough)

Teacher activities

- Screen a five-minute extract of the walkthrough. Ask learners to write notes on how they interpret the game.
- Ask learners to consider how different audiences might interpret that same walkthrough (perhaps allocate learners an audience type, such as parent, grandparent, teenager, five-year-old child).
- Facilitate class discussion of the expectation for merchandising, such as video games, to accompany the release of major films.
- Ensure that learners understand that Time Warner is a global media conglomerate funded commercially, owned by shareholders, that uses film as a prestige product to sell convergent products.
- Introduce the homework task.

Learner activities

- Learners view the walkthrough, making notes on their personal reaction to the extract of the game.
- Learners view the walkthrough again, attempting to make notes on how an audience member of a different age or gender might view the game.
- As a class, learners discuss different personal reactions. They consider how they might expect other social groups to interpret the game.
- Individually, learners write a statement that explains which age group they feel the game is best suited to, giving examples from the walkthroughs they have seen and three reasons for their choice of age group.
- As a class, learners debate the view that nowadays we accept and expect merchandising as an integral part of a film becoming a cultural event.
- In pairs, learners plan a way to collate data for the homework task. They anticipate the types of results that they expect to find.

Suggested homework

Learners visit a supermarket and conduct a mini-research project on the number and nature of products linked to major films.

Year 2 Week 6a

Television – crime drama

Learning objectives – learners will be able to:

- analyse extracts in terms of media language and representations
- explain the influence of patriarchy and feminism (or post-feminism) on representations in *Cuffs*
- explain the influence of multiculturalism on representations in *Cuffs*
- explain the influence of changing attitudes to sexualities on representations in *Cuffs*.

Key products

Cuffs, Series 1, Episode 1, BBC1
Cuffs, Series 1, Episode 7, BBC1

Teacher activities

- Put learners into groups of four, giving each group a large A3 sheet with an area of media language on it. Give learners one minute to brainstorm as many elements of the media language element as they can remember. After one minute, move the A3 sheet on to the next table and ask learners to use a different colour to add to the previous group's brainstorm. Repeat until each group has contributed to brainstorms for each of the four media language elements.
- Ask a learner from each group to feed back one or two elements from each brainstorm.
- Lead a recap of the conventions of crime drama, referring back to lessons 12a and 12b in Year 1.
- Screen two sequences from a chosen episode of *Cuffs*.
- Give learners a brief introduction to the social and cultural contexts that the unit focuses on, including feminism and multiculturalism, and how these can affect the way in which groups are represented in television crime drama. Encourage learners to identify what effects this could have and to make links to anything observed in the episode and sequences watched.
- Place learners in pairs and ask them to identify key scenes from the episode(s) studied that provide evidence for changing attitudes to sexuality, multiculturalism and feminism.

Learner activities

- Individually, learners contribute to group brainstorms revising key media language terms of camerawork, editing, mise-en-scène and sound.
- Learners identify four conventions of television crime drama present in the sequences from *Cuffs*.
- In pairs, learners identify three key scenes from the specified episode of *Cuffs* which show changing attitudes to sexuality, evidence of patriarchy or multiculturalism.

Suggested homework

Learners watch one other crime drama and compare the social issues it explores with those in *Cuffs*.

Year 2 Week 6b

Television – crime drama

> ### Learning objectives – learners will be able to:
>
> - explain the dominance of the crime drama in contemporary television due to its potential to explore social issues in an accessible way
> - explain how increasing competition for television is driving the search for programmes that engage audience loyalty with serial narratives.

Key products

Television listings such as those found at http://www.radiotimes.com/

Teacher activities

- Direct learners to brainstorm all crime dramas that they have watched. Record a list on the board.
- Ask learners to discuss why these programmes are popular with audiences.
- Give out an example of television schedules for a week.
- Put learners into pairs or threes and give each pair/three a channel to investigate. Ask them to identify, using a coloured highlighter, where in the schedule any television crime programme is placed.
- Direct group feedback, recording on the board similarities in day of week and time of day for crime drama scheduling. Discuss possible reasons for this scheduling, including the popular Sunday evening slot and mid-week post-watershed slots, and why crime drama is so popular with audiences.
- Direct learners to identify, using a different highlighter, the next most popular genres of programme in the schedules (such as comedy or game shows) as a point of comparison. Ask them to see whether any similarities occur between the scheduling of these genres and to identify competition for crime drama.
- Lead a discussion focusing on how Netflix and Amazon Prime are competing with television channels to bring crime drama to an audience that craves them.
- Set a small writing activity: 'Why are television crime dramas popular with audiences?'

Learner activities

- Learners identify at least two reasons why crime dramas are popular with audiences and contribute to class discussion.
- Learners identify the scheduling of popular television crime dramas and draw conclusions as to the reasons for the choices made, including why they dominate the schedules compared with most other genres.
- Learners respond individually to the small writing activity.

Year 2 Week 7a

Television – crime drama: regulation

Learning objectives – learners will be able to:

- explain the role of Ofcom in the regulation of television
- state the requirements of the BBC's PSB remit
- explain the BBC charter, 'Reithian' values and their influence on programming.

Key product

Inside the BBC (http://www.bbc.co.uk/aboutthebbc/insidethebbc/whoweare)

Teacher activities

- Introduce the class to the BBC. Identify what learners already know about the BBC, its values and vision and how it is regulated. Explain how Ofcom regulates commercial television and why the BBC is regulated via a process of self-governance.
- Set the learners a small group research task to find out the following information using the 'Inside the BBC' webpage: public service broadcasting (PSB); the BBC's mission, values and vision; the BBC's public purpose (BBC Charter); where the licence fee goes; and the history of the BBC. Each group should research and present on a separate area following a series of guided questions. Research could be presented visually and kept for revision purposes.
- Facilitate learner feedback on their research.
- Using schedule lists for BBC 1, BBC 2 and BBC 4 (available on iPlayer), ask learners to identify which programmes represent elements of the BBC's mission to educate, entertain and inform.
- Lead plenary discussion reflecting on the function and role of the BBC.

Learner activities

- In pairs, learners complete a research activity using the BBC's 'Inside the BBC' webpage. They collate their research and present it visually using Prezi, PowerPoint or similar.
- Individually, learners identify at least one example of a BBC programme from the schedules provided that it illustrates an element or elements of the BBC mission statement.

Year 2 Week 7b

Television – crime drama

Learning objectives – learners will be able to:
● discuss how *Cuffs* meets PSB requirements
● state how the BBC uses its digital platform to create convergence.

Key products

Inside the BBC (http://www.bbc.co.uk/aboutthebbc/insidethebbc/whoweare)

Article on BBC Three's move online (http://www.bbc.co.uk/newsbeat/article/33332280/everything-you-need-to-know-about-bbc-threes-move-online)

Teacher activities

● Lead a recap with learners on the BBC and its role in PSB broadcasting (Lesson 7a).

● Divide learners into small groups or pairs. Ask them to identify features from *Cuffs* that fit the remit and ethos of the BBC and any elements or features that challenge it.

● Lead an exposition focusing on how BBC television channels have to balance the needs and demands of an audience with following the BBC's remit, using the demise of BBC Three as a television channel as an example. Ask learners what they know about BBC Three, its origins and why it was moved online.

● Get learners individually to read the online article about the move of BBC Three online. Explain the key term convergence and show how BBC Three is an example of this.

● Direct learners to look at BBC Three on the BBC iPlayer and to identify a range of different programmes aired. Compare with the programme make-up for BBC 1 and BBC 4.

Learner activities

● Learners note down four features of *Cuffs* that fit the remit and ethos of the BBC and at least one feature that challenges them.

● Individually, learners read through the online article on the demise of BBC Three and make notes on the reasons for the decision to remove it from the television schedules. They categorise the reasons under 'audience' and 'industry'.

● Learners look at the range of programmes offered by BBC channels on iPlayer and choose contrasting programmes to show how the programme mix fits every element of the BBC remit.

Suggested homework

Learners produce a PowerPoint presentation showing how the BBC is responding to differing audience tastes through its programme mix and available platforms.

Year 2 Week 8a

Television – crime drama

Learning objectives – learners will be able to:

- analyse the social groups present in and absent from *The Avengers*
- discuss the reasons for this presence/absence
- discuss the use of stereotypes (and/or anti-stereotypes) in *The Avengers* – especially gender stereotypes
- analyse the messages and values in *The Avengers*.

Key product

The Avengers, Series 4, Episode 1, ITV

Teacher activities

- Provide contextual background to the programme (set product), including the main character names, a brief overview of the narrative being established and where the episode is set.
- Pair up learners and give each learner a different area of focus to make notes on during the screening, choosing from characters or narrative/storylines.
- Screen the whole one-hour episode of *The Avengers*.
- Ask learners briefly to identify any obvious stereotypes or anti-stereotypes found in the episode of *The Avengers*, focusing in particular on how gender is represented.

Learner activities

- Learners make notes in their exercise books on the background and context to the key product *The Avengers*.
- In pairs, learners make detailed notes on their assigned area during the screening of the episode, in preparation for discussion work in the next lesson.
- Learners identify at least one stereotype and one anti-stereotype found in the episode.

Year 2 Week 8b

Television – crime drama

Learning objectives – learners will be able to:

- analyse the social groups present in and absent from *The Avengers*
- discuss the reasons for this presence/absence
- discuss the use of stereotypes in *The Avengers*
- analyse the messages and values in *The Avengers*.

Key product

Digitised (if possible) sequences from **The Avengers**, Series 4, Episode 1, ITV

Teacher activities

- Briefly recap the narrative from the screening of *The Avengers* in Lesson 8a.
- Ask learners to create a character list, identifying elements of character including gender, ethnicity, age range and other relevant social groups. Learners could do this individually and feed back as a jigsaw exercise.
- Lead a discussion about which social groups or stereotypes are absent, being challenged and being reinforced in the episode. Encourage learners to consider reasons why this may be so.
- Assign pairs/threes a character and ask learners to identify and present a key sequence from the screened episode of *The Avengers* in which their character either challenges or conforms to expected stereotypes.
- Ask learners to plot their profiled character on a narrative arc, mapping how they interact with other elements of the narrative and other characters.

Learner activities

- Learners build a profile of their assigned character or characters. They present the character to the rest of the class.
- In pairs or threes, learners identify a second sequence from the episode which demonstrates stereotypes being conformed to or challenged, and present this sequence to the class.
- In small groups, learners plot the character they profiled earlier on a narrative arc, mapping how they interact with other elements of the narrative and other characters.

Suggested homework

Learners watch at least one other episode of *The Avengers* online.

Year 2 Week 9a

Television – crime drama

Learning objectives – learners will be able to:

- explain how representations of gender, sexuality and ethnicity reflect historical and contemporary social and cultural contexts in *Cuffs* and *The Avengers*.

Key products

The Avengers, Series 4, Episode 1, ITV

Cuffs, Series 1, Episode 1, BBC1

British Library teaching resources on the history of feminism in Britain for reference purposes (https://www.bl.uk/sisterhood/teaching-resources)

The 'Women's Timeline' (Manchester University) (https://www.mmu.ac.uk/equality-and-diversity/doc/gender-equality-timeline.pdf)

Teacher activities

- Give learners a brief introduction to changing gender roles in the 1960s and what this meant for the way women began to be represented in media products. Focus on pre-1970s feminism but post-'sexual revolution' representations. Introduce other key areas of context: multiculturalism and sexuality.

- Direct learners to plot on a timeline the significant changes that occurred for women in the early to late 1960s.

- Ask learners to compare how female characters are represented in both key products and to draw contrasts between the UK in the 1960s and present day. Learners should be assigned a different character and feed back through a presentation or jigsaw feedback to a different group. Ensure that learners include the key areas of ethnicity and sexuality in their analysis.

- Ask learners to compare how male characters are represented in both key products and to draw conclusions. Ensure that learners include the key areas of ethnicity and sexuality in their analysis.

- Facilitate feedback to a class discussion focusing on the similarities and differences between representations in the key products and how these reflect the time in which the products were set.

Learner activities

- Learners individually plot key moments in the 1960s on their timeline.

- In groups of three, learners identify key areas of representation for two female characters (one from each product) including ethnicity, sexuality, age and job. They contribute to a feedback discussion.

- In groups of three, learners repeat the task above for male characters.

- Learners draw conclusions and make contributions to a class discussion focusing on how the representations in the programmes reflect the time in which they were set.

Year 2 Week 9b

Television – contexts

Learning objectives – learners will be able to:

- explain how representations in television programmes reflect historical and contemporary social and cultural contexts
- consider the effect of different audience expectations on how audiences from different times might interpret different representations.

Key products

BBC 'On This Day' archive (http://news.bbc.co.uk/onthisday/hi/themes/world_politics/cold_war/default.stm)

The National Archives teaching resources (http://www.nationalarchives.gov.uk/education/resources/sixties-britain/)

The Avengers, Series 4, Episode 1, ITV

Cuffs, Series 1, Episode 1, BBC1

Teacher activities

- Using selected resources from the National Archives and the BBC 'On This Day' archive, assign groups of three a resource and ask them to summarise what the main threats to social order in the UK were in the 1960s. Choose a range of resources from different moments in the decade.
- Direct learners to place their summary on a timeline on the floor.
- Facilitate feedback to the board, identifying similarities between key areas, including fear of spies, threats of outsiders, paranoia of the 'other'.
- Introduce the idea that what goes on in society will affect the content of television programmes and that the content of *The Avengers* will meet the needs of a 1960s audience.
- In pairs, direct learners to identify key moments in *The Avengers* that demonstrate these ideas. Ask pairs to feed back to another pair and to discuss what this suggests about audience expectations of representations in the programme.
- Lead class feedback, encouraging learners to think about how an audience from the twenty-first century may interpret these representations differently – would they recognise the same threats?
- Direct learners to think about how an audience from the 1960s might interpret representations from the episode of *Cuffs* differently from an audience from the 2010s. Individually, learners identify the main threats in the episode and consider how different audiences would interpret this differently.

Learner activities

- In pairs, learners create a bullet-point summary of a moment in 1960s history.
- Learners identify two key moments from *The Avengers* which illustrate contexts.
- Learners compare audience interpretations from the 1960s and the 2010s.

Suggested homework

Learners write an essay in response to the question: 'How do television programmes reflect different historical contexts? Use *The Avengers* and *Cuffs* to illustrate your answer.'

Year 2 Week 10a

Television – crime drama

Learning objectives – learners will be able to:

- analyse camerawork and sound in sequences from *The Avengers*
- suggest connotations for examples of media language used.

Key product

Key sequences from *The Avengers*, Series 4, Episode 1, ITV

Teacher activities

- As learners arrive in class ask them to write one camerawork term and one sound term on separate sticky notes and stick them on the board. Use the sticky notes as a revision activity to test learners' knowledge and understanding of the terms through question and answer (e.g. 'Describe a pan', 'What is a sound motif?').
- Screen a selected sequence from Episode 1, Series 4, of *The Avengers* three times, with short note-making breaks between each screening.
- Divide learners into groups of four. Direct one pair to analyse the use of camerawork and the other pair to analyse the use of sound, encouraging them to focus on connotations created.
- Facilitate learner feedback.
- Set a timed writing exercise: 'How is media language used to create meaning in the opening sequence?'

Learner activities

- Learners write one camerawork term and one sound term on separate sticky notes and stick them on the board at the front of the class. Learners participate in a question and answer revision activity.
- Learners watch the selected sequence from Episode 1, Series 4, of *The Avengers* again and individually make notes on a new area of media language.
- Learners share their findings with a partner before sharing with the class.
- Learners complete the timed writing activity (10 minutes).

Year 2 Week 10b

Television – crime drama

Learning objectives – learners will be able to:

- analyse editing and mise-en-scène in sequences from *The Avengers*
- suggest connotations for examples of media language used
- state any examples of intertexuality that exist in the product.

Key product

Key sequences from *The Avengers*, Series 4, Episode 1, ITV

Teacher activities

- Screen a selected sequence from Episode 1, Series 4, of *The Avengers* three times, with short note-making breaks between each screening.
- Put students into groups of four. Direct one pair to analyse the use of editing and the other pair to analyse the use of mise-en-scène in creating meaning in the sequence.
- Direct learner feedback.
- Remind learners of the definition of the term 'intertextual'. Direct learners to discuss in small groups any examples of intertextuality found in *The Avengers*.

Learner activities

- Learners watch the sequence from Episode 1, Series 4, of *The Avengers* and individually identify and make notes on a designated area of media language.
- Learners share their findings with a partner before sharing with the class.
- Learners identify one example of intertextuality found in *The Avengers*.

Suggested homework

Learners watch the opening sequence to a second episode of *The Avengers*. They analyse the use of media language in creating meaning for an audience. They identify at least one use of each of the four technical areas of camerawork, editing, mise-en-scène and sound. They then write up the analysis in approximately 200 words.

Year 2 Week 11a

Television – crime drama

Learning objectives – learners will be able to:

- state the generic conventions of the spy drama genre and exemplify using *The Avengers*
- explain how the episode of *The Avengers* creates the narrative resolution required for a series narrative
- compare the narrative in *The Avengers* with that of *Cuffs*.

Key products

The Avengers, Series 4, Episode 1, ITV

Cuffs, Series 1, Episode 1, BBC1

Teacher activities

- Lead a recap of the conventions of crime drama, inviting learners to contribute to a class brainstorm on the board.
- Ask learners to identify which of these conventions is found in the spy genre through reference to *The Avengers*.
- Briefly recap the narrative of *The Avengers* episode studied in Lesson 8a.
- In pairs, get learners to plot the narrative arc of *The Avengers* on an axis.
- Remind learners of the definitions of 'series' and 'serial'.
- Ask learners to compare the narrative structure of *Cuffs* with that of *The Avengers*, with *Cuffs* being an example of a serial and *The Avengers* having a narrative ending in keeping with a series.
- Facilitate feedback.
- Set a timed writing exercise: 'Compare how narrative resolution is established in *The Avengers* and *Cuffs*.'

Learner activities

- Learners identify at least three conventions of the crime drama.
- Learners identify at least two conventions of the spy drama.
- In pairs and using an axis/graph, learners plot the narrative development of the episode of *The Avengers* studied in Lesson 8a, noting which parts of the narrative reach a conclusion and whether there are any strands of the narrative left unfinished.
- Learners compare the narrative strands and arc found in the episode of *Cuffs* studied.
- Learners feed back their findings to class discussion.
- Learners complete the timed writing activity.

Year 2 Week 11b

Television – crime drama

> ## Learning objectives – learners will be able to:
> - state Propp's character categories: villain, hero, princess, donor, helper, dispatcher, false hero
> - exemplify Propp's character categories through reference to both *The Avengers* and *Cuffs*.

Key product

Opening 7 minutes to *Star Wars Episode IV* (https://www.youtube.com/watch?v=yHfLyMAHrQE)

Teacher activities

- Screen the opening sequence from *Star Wars Episode IV*.
- Ask learners to note down the main characters from the film.
- Introduce Propp's character categories and the theory behind his ideas.
- Ask learners to identify which of the characters from *Star Wars* fits which character category. Discuss how this helps us to understand the narrative.
- Direct learners to identify a second film to which they can apply the theory.
- Lead a discussion focusing on how Propp's character categories can be used to help identify characters in television too.
- Put learners into pairs and ask them to identify use of Propp's character categories in both *Cuffs* and *The Avengers*.
- Facilitate learner discussion focusing on similarities and differences between characters in both products.

Learner activities

- Learners watch the opening to *Star Wars Episode IV* and identify all the main characters.
- Learners use Propp's theory to categorise the main characters.
- In pairs, learners identify how characters in both *Cuffs* and *The Avengers* can be categorised in the same way using Propp's theory.

Suggested homework

Short essay: 'How far do *Cuffs* and *The Avengers* tell similar stories to be popular with mass audiences?'

Year 2 Week 12a

Television – crime drama

Learning objectives – learners will be able to:

- outline and compare the uses and gratifications offered by *Cuffs* and *The Avengers*.

Key products

Overview of the uses and gratifications theory (http://www.bbc.co.uk/education/guides/zg24frd/revision/3)

Television listings (http://www.radiotimes.com/tv/tv-listings/)

Teacher activities

- Review the uses and gratifications theory.
- Direct learners individually to identify an example of a media product for each category and then an example of a television programme in the schedules for each category.
- Facilitate feedback.
- Put learners in pairs and direct them to identify elements of the uses and gratifications theory offered by both *Cuffs* and *The Avengers*.
- Help learners to draw comparisons between the programmes and conclusions from this.
- Direct learners, in pairs, to create an infographic which illustrates how the uses and gratifications theory can be applied to both *Cuffs* and *The Avengers*.

Learner activities

- Individually, learners identify an example of a media product and a television programme from the schedules to illustrate all four areas of the uses and gratifications theory.
- In pairs, learners identify four ways that *Cuffs* and *The Avengers* fit the uses and gratifications theory.
- In pairs, learners create an infographic. They share it with the class and keep for revision purposes.

Year 2 Week 12b

Television – crime drama

> ### Learning objectives – learners will be able to:
> - explain how ITV targets both a prime-time adult British audience and international sales
> - state the dominance of ITV as the only commercial channel in the three-channel 1960s.

Key products

The *TV Times* Archive (https://radiosoundsfamiliar.com/the-tv-times-archive-1960s.php)

The *Avengers* Forever: how *The Avengers* went international (http://theavengers.tv/forever/peel1-prod.htm)

Teacher activities

- Contextualise television in the UK in the 1960s. Explain the limited choice for audiences due to the limited number of channels and that ITV was the only commercial channel available at this time.
- Project a copy of an ITV schedule from November 1965.
- Ask learners to explore the types of programmes available. Direct them to link the programme mix to the influence of public service broadcasting (PSB) on ITV schedules. Compare this with the programme mix found in today's schedules.
- Direct learners to identify the scheduling for *The Avengers*.
- Lead a discussion focusing on how *The Avengers* fits its schedule of prime-time (9.05pm, Saturday) post-watershed and how this appeals to a mass audience.
- Ask learners to research the background to the selling of *The Avengers* to an international market.
- If time allows, direct learners to work in pairs to take on the role of a television scheduler and create a day schedule for BBC 1 in 1965 and ITV in 2018.

Learner activities

- Using the 1965 television schedule, learners identify at least four different genres of television programme. They compare these with those found in today's schedules and draw conclusions.
- Learners show how the PSB mix (news, current affairs, classical music, single plays, etc.) influences the commercial channel programme mix in the 1960s by picking relevant programmes from the schedules.
- Learners identify the schedule for *The Avengers* and explain why it fits this day and time, along with the appeal for a mass audience.
- Learners complete the small research activity identifying reasons for the change to the fourth series to suit an international market.
- Learners work in pairs to create a schedule for one channel in one year.

Suggested homework

Short essay: 'Explore the uses and gratifications of television dramas. Use one programme you have studied to illustrate your answer.'

Year 2 Week 13a

Radio – media industries

> ### Learning objectives – learners will be able to:
>
> - identify the regulator for radio
> - identify different types of radio station: international (e.g. the World Service), national and local broadcast, online, commercial and public service broadcasting.

Introduction

The work on radio relates to Section A: Music for the assessment Music and News (02), the written exam paper. Radio must be studied in relation to media industries and media audiences.

Key products

BBC Annual Report and Accounts 2016/17 (https://downloads.bbc.co.uk/aboutthebbc/insidethebbc/reports/pdf/bbc-annualreport-201617.pdf)

Wikipedia entry for commercial broadcasting (https://en.wikipedia.org/wiki/Commercial_broadcasting)

What is Ofcom? (https://www.ofcom.org.uk/about-ofcom/what-is-ofcom)

Teacher activities

- Recap the media audience comparison and contrast of *The Avengers* and *Cuffs* from the previous session.
- Introduce the area of study and put it into the context of the examination.
- Give learners a list of key media industries and audience terms for radio, including: ownership and control, convergence, funding, globalised audiences, regulation, target audience, marketing, active audiences, uses and gratifications.
- Display 'What is Ofcom?' for a whole-class lecture, explaining that it is the radio regulator.

Learner activities

- Learners take notes following set questions on Ofcom.
- In pairs, learners research different types of radio station, including online commercial stations, broadcast commercial radio (on Wikipedia) and PSB BBC stations on iPlayer. It may be helpful to give learners a list of research sources (see above) and a table to aid their research.
- Learners contribute to class feedback using the notes they have made.

Suggested homework

Learners listen to three BBC radio stations they have not previously accessed and note the differences in style and content.

Year 2 Week 13b

Radio – media audiences and contexts

Learning objectives – learners will be able to:

- identify the target audience for BBC Radios 1 to 6 in terms of their content
- state which BBC radio channels best meet PSB requirements
- state the outlines of the political debate as to whether or not Radio 1 should be privatised.

Key products

BBC Annual Report and Accounts 2016/17 (https://downloads.bbc.co.uk/aboutthebbc/insidethebbc/reports/pdf/bbc-annualreport-201617.pdf)

BBC Trust Radio service licences (http://www.bbc.co.uk/bbctrust/our_work/services/radio/service_licences.html)

The origins of BBC local radio (http://www.bbc.co.uk/historyofthebbc/research/general/local-radio)

Teacher activities

- Ask learners, using computers, to make notes on the BBC radio stations in terms of audiences, content and PSB requirements. The BBC Annual Report and Accounts 2016/17 and the BBC Trust Radio service licences website could be helpful resources.
- Set the task for learners to answer the following question, making written notes: 'Radio 3 has a small audience yet a large budget, but its existence is never questioned by politicians, while Radio 1 is attacked as "too commercial". Is this fair?'
- Facilitate a whole-class discussion, encouraging learners to try out media industries and audience terms (e.g. regulation and ownership). Learners should decide whether or not Radio 1 should be privatised.

Learner activities

- In pairs, learners research the target audiences and content for BBC Radio stations 1–6 using the BBC Annual Report and Accounts 2016/17 (page 27) and examine how the descriptions of each channel emphasise its PSB elements.
- Learners explore how effectively the BBC reaches all audiences with its radio stations, making written notes. It may be helpful to give them a table to complete.
- Learners feed back their findings to the whole class.

Suggested homework

Learners write a short proposal for a new digital BBC radio station targeted at 6–12 year olds, emphasising the PSB elements.

Year 2 Week 14a

BBC Radio 1 Live Lounge – media audiences

Learning objectives – learners will be able to:

- state the target audience for Radio 1
- suggest the uses and gratifications offered by BBC Radio 1 *Live Lounge*
- suggest how audiences might interpret BBC Radio 1 *Live Lounge* differently depending on fandom.

Key products

Live Lounge, **BBC Radio 1**, centre-selected episode, freely available online via BBC Radio iPlayer (http://www.bbc.co.uk/programmes/p01029mq)

Uses and gratifications theory (http://communicationtheory.org/uses-and-gratification-theory/)

Additional resources

BBC Radio 1 *Live Lounge* (http://www.bbc.co.uk/programmes/p01029mq)

BBC Radio 1 *Live Lounge* **archive** (https://www.bbc.co.uk/events/rnc5d4/by/date/2015)

More From Radio 1's *Live Lounge* (https://www.youtube.com/playlist?list=PL1CA6335E0D3699B6)

Teacher activities

- Recap key media industries and audiences terms for radio, including: ownership and control, convergence, funding, globalised audiences, regulation, target audience, marketing, active audiences, uses and gratifications.
- Display Radio 1 *Live Lounge* webpage for whole-class analysis, focusing on the target audience (e.g. PSB, uses and gratifications, availability, styles and/or genres played, eras of programming, how producers of radio programmes may target audiences through other services, and brand image).
- Direct whole-class analysis and discussion of the uses and gratifications theory and Radio 1 *Live Lounge*, encouraging learners to try out and apply the key terms.

Learner activities

- In pairs, learners use computers to research the uses and gratifications theory and discuss how it can be applied to different BBC radio stations.
- As a class, learners discuss and analyse media audience, making notes, in terms of the Radio 1 *Live Lounge* target audience. They learn to apply the correct terminology (e.g. the role of gender, age, fandom, etc.).
- Learners contribute to class feedback using the notes they have made.

Suggested homework

Learners write up their media audience analysis of Radio 1 *Live Lounge* from the lesson.

Year 2 Week 14b

Radio 1 *Live Lounge* – media audiences

Learning objectives – learners will be able to:

- identify and discuss how Radio 1 *Live Lounge* uses BBC iPlayer to reach audiences
- explain how Radio 1 *Live Lounge* tries to fit the BBC's PSB requirements.

Key products

Live Lounge, BBC Radio 1, centre-selected episode, freely available online via BBC Radio iPlayer (http://www.bbc.co.uk/programmes/p01029mq)

BBC Radio 1 *Live Lounge* (http://www.bbc.co.uk/programmes/p01029mq)

BBC Radio 1 *Live Lounge* archive (https://www.bbc.co.uk/events/rnc5d4/by/date/2015)

More From Radio 1's *Live Lounge* (https://www.youtube.com/playlist?list=PL1CA6335E0D3699B6)

Teacher activities

- Display the Radio 1 *Live Lounge* webpage for whole-class analysis, focusing on media audiences (e.g. PSB, uses and gratifications, availability, styles and/or genres played, eras of programming, how producers of radio programmes may target audiences through other services, and brand image).
- Direct whole-class discussion on how Radio 1 *Live Lounge* uses BBC iPlayer to reach audiences, encouraging learners to try out and apply key terms.
- Facilitate review discussion of BBC radio stations.

Learner activities

- In pairs, learners discuss and research why producers of radio programmes target different audiences, making notes (e.g. targeting an otherwise unserved niche audience in order to compete in the market; targeting a mass audience to sell to advertisers; targeting a well-defined niche audience to sell to advertisers; as part of a PSB requirement to address a specific audience on the channel). It may be helpful to give learners a list of questions to aid their research.
- Learners feed back their findings to the whole class. Ensure that discussion focuses on how far the choice of presenter, the choice of music played and the emphasis on live performance fulfils the BBC's PSB requirement to be distinctive, to reflect diversity within the UK, to create innovative and challenging content, and to serve all audiences.

Suggested homework

Learners write an essay: 'How does BBC music radio fulfil the BBC's PSB requirements to be distinctive, to reflect diversity within the UK, to create innovative and challenging content, and to serve all audiences? Refer to the *Live Lounge* in your answer.'

Year 2 Week 15a

Music videos – media language and media representations

> ### Learning objectives – learners will be able to:
>
> - explain the influence of patriarchy and feminism (or post-feminism) on representations in the chosen set music videos
> - explain the influence of multiculturalism on representations in the chosen set music videos
> - explain the influence of changing attitudes to sexualities on representations in the chosen set music videos.

Key products

Learners need to study **one set pair** of music videos from the list below:

1. **Wheatus, *Teenage Dirtbag*** (https://www.youtube.com/watch?v=FC3y9llDXuM) and **Avril Lavigne, *Sk8er Boi*** (https://www.youtube.com/watch?v=TIy3n2b7V9k)

2. **Mark Ronson feat. Bruno Mars, *Uptown Funk*** (https://www.youtube.com/watch?v=OPf0YbXqDm0) and **Beyoncé, *If I Were A Boy*** (https://www.youtube.com/watch?v=AWpsOqh8q0M)

3. **The Vamps feat. Demi Lovato, *Somebody To You*** (https://www.youtube.com/watch?v=0go2nfVXFgA) and **Little Mix, *Black Magic*** (https://www.youtube.com/watch?v=MkElfR_NPBI)

4. **Tinie Tempah feat. Jess Glynne, *Not Letting Go*** (https://www.youtube.com/watch?v=nsDwItoNlLc) and **Paloma Faith, *Picking Up the Pieces*** (https://www.youtube.com/watch?v=Ijel4Vcqd9g)

Additional resources

Huffington Post 'Gender Roles in Media' (http://www.huffingtonpost.com/allison-lantagne/gender-roles-media_b_5326199.html)

USC Annenberg Media 'Gender Gap in Music' (http://www.uscannenbergmedia.com/2017/01/26/gender-gap-in-music/)

Teacher activities

- Recap media audience analysis of Radio 1 *Live Lounge*, including: availability, styles and/or genres played, eras of programming, how producers of radio programmes may target audiences through other services, and brand image.
- Recap the set music videos, focusing on media language and representation.
- Screen set music videos (if required).
- Direct whole-class analysis and discussion of the representation of gender, race/ethnicity and sexualities in the set music videos in relation to social contexts.

Learner activities

- Using computers in small groups, learners research media representations in the set music videos (e.g. patriarchy, feminism, multiculturalism, changing attitudes to sexualities). It may be helpful to give them a list of questions to aid their research.
- Learners contribute to a whole-class discussion and analysis of media representations in the set music videos, learning to apply the correct terminology.
- Learners feed back their findings to the whole class.

Suggested homework

Learners complete an extended essay: 'How do fans of music artists use their fandom to help construct an identity? Provide examples.'

Year 2 Week 15b

Music videos – media audiences and contexts

Learning objectives – learners will be able to:

- explain the influence of the dominance of celebrity culture on the chosen set music videos
- suggest how audiences might interpret music videos differently depending on gender, age and fandom
- explain how fans of music artists may use their fandom to help construct an identity (e.g. through a sense of belonging).

Key products

Learners need to study **one set pair** of music videos from the list below:

1. **Wheatus, *Teenage Dirtbag*** (https://www.youtube.com/watch?v=FC3y9llDXuM) and **Avril Lavigne, *Sk8er Boi*** (https://www.youtube.com/watch?v=TIy3n2b7V9k)

2. **Mark Ronson feat. Bruno Mars, *Uptown Funk*** (https://www.youtube.com/watch?v=OPf0YbXqDm0) and **Beyoncé, *If I Were A Boy*** (https://www.youtube.com/watch?v=AWpsOqh8q0M)

3. **The Vamps feat. Demi Lovato, *Somebody To You*** (https://www.youtube.com/watch?v=0go2nfVXFgA) and **Little Mix, *Black Magic*** (https://www.youtube.com/watch?v=MkElfR_NPBI)

4. **Tinie Tempah feat. Jess Glynne, *Not Letting Go*** (https://www.youtube.com/watch?v=nsDwItoNlLc) and **Paloma Faith, *Picking Up the Pieces*** (https://www.youtube.com/watch?v=Ijel4Vcqd9g)

Additional resources

Huffington Post 'Gender Roles in Media' (http://www.huffingtonpost.com/allison-lantagne/gender-roles-media_b_5326199.html)

USC Annenberg Media 'Gender Gap in Music' (http://www.uscannenbergmedia.com/2017/01/26/gender-gap-in-music/)

BBC Bitesize, GCSE Media Studies – Target audience (http://www.bbc.co.uk/education/guides/zy24p39/revision)

Teacher activities

- Direct whole-class discussion of how far each music video is influenced by celebrity culture (e.g. in the emphasis on the performer and performance rather than the song) and the role of the music video in promoting celebrity culture.
- Set a timed writing exercise: 'How do fans of music artists use their fandom to help construct an identity?'

Learner activities

- As a class, learners discuss the role of gender, age and fandom within the set music videos. It may be helpful to give them a list of questions.
- In small groups, learners discuss and make notes on how far they identify with artists or feel they belong to a fan group and why this may be particularly significant for young people exploring their place in the world.
- Learners contribute to class feedback using the notes they have made.
- Learners complete the timed writing activity.

Suggested homework

Learners write up their notes from the lesson on celebrity culture and write an essay: 'Analyse the representations in one music video you have studied, including in relation to its social and cultural contexts.'

Year 2 Week 16a

Music magazines – media representations

Learning objectives – learners will be able to:

- explain the influence of popular music from previous decades on media representations, particularly those aimed at older audiences
- explain the influence of gender roles in popular music on media representations.

Key products

Centres need at least two magazines so that learners can study one whole edition and at least two covers.

MOJO magazine

Music magazine alternative

Additional resources

The official MOJO magazine YouTube channel (https://www.youtube.com/user/MOJO4MUSIC)

MOJO magazine homepage (http://www.mojo4music.com/)

BBC News, 'Baby boom ... and bust' (http://news.bbc.co.uk/1/hi/magazine/4798825.stm)

Teacher activities

- Recap the differences in audience interpretations of the set music videos from the previous session, including gender, age and fandom.
- Recap MOJO magazine, focusing on media language and representation in relation to its social and cultural contexts (e.g. the influence of popular music from previous decades on media representations, particularly those aimed at older audiences).
- Display MOJO magazine (if required).

Learner activities

- Using computers, learners research and design a popular music timeline showcasing media representations from different decades.
- As a class, learners discuss the influence of gender roles in popular music, learning to apply the correct terminology.
- Learners contribute to a class discussion using the notes they have made.

Suggested homework

Learners write up their notes on the influence of gender roles in popular music on media representations from the lesson. Then they write an extended essay: 'How do the music magazines you have studied use media representations in the same way and differently?'

Year 2 Week 16b

Music magazines – media representations and contexts

Learning objectives – learners will be able to:

- explain the influence of racial and ethnic affiliations on representations of different types of popular music
- analyse the influence of contexts on *MOJO* front covers.

Key products

Centres need at least two magazines so that learners can study one whole edition and at least two covers.

MOJO magazine

Music magazine alternative

Additional resources

The official *MOJO* magazine YouTube channel (https://www.youtube.com/user/MOJO4MUSIC)

MOJO magazine homepage (http://www.mojo4music.com/)

MOJO magazine latest issue and cover archive (http://www.mojo4music.com/magazine/)

CityLab 'The Geography of Pop Music Superstars' (https://www.citylab.com/life/2015/08/the-geography-of-pop-music-superstars/402445/)

Teacher activities

- Display CityLab 'The Geography of Pop Music Superstars' for whole-class discussion. Focus on the influence of racial and ethnic affiliations on representations of different types of popular music. Learners take notes following set questions.
- Direct a whole-class discussion on the influence of contexts on media representations (such as the high esteem afforded 'classic rock' by the baby-boomer generation; the largely sexist roles offered to women within that musical genre; the dominance of white British and American musicians in that genre).

Learner activities

- In pairs, learners complete an in-depth analysis and make notes on the influence of contexts on two *MOJO* front covers. Learners complete a further comparison study of one other front cover from a different genre of music. It may be helpful to give learners a table or a list of questions to aid their analysis.
- Learners feed back their findings to the whole class.

Suggested homework

Learners write an essay: 'Analyse the representations in one music magazine you have studied, including in relation to its social and cultural contexts.'

Year 2 Week 17a

Music magazines – media industries

> ### Learning objectives – learners will be able to:
> - identify the funding for *MOJO* magazine
> - identify that the newspaper and magazine industries can choose to be self-regulated
> - explain how *MOJO* uses convergence through its website.

Key products

Centres need at least two magazines so that learners can study one whole edition and at least two covers.

MOJO magazine

Music magazine alternative

MOJO magazine homepage (http://www.mojo4music.com/)

Independent Press Standards Organisation (IPSO) (https://www.ipso.co.uk/about-ipso/who-ipso-regulates/?letters=m)

Additional resources

The official *MOJO* magazine YouTube channel (https://www.youtube.com/user/MOJO4MUSIC)

Teacher activities

- Recap the influence of social/cultural contexts on music magazines and the influence of media representations in *MOJO* magazine from the previous session.
- Display the homepage of IPSO, the self-regulator for *MOJO*, for whole-class discussion. Learners take notes following set questions.
- Give learners a definition of convergence and ask them to search for examples on the *MOJO* website.

Learner activities

- As a class, learners discuss magazine regulation, focusing on non-independent regulation.
- In pairs, learners research the *MOJO* website and make notes. They discuss the uses and gratifications offered generally by magazines and specifically by *MOJO*. It may be helpful to give them a list of questions to aid their analysis.
- Learners feed back their findings to the whole class.

Suggested homework

Learners write up their media industries notes on IPSO for *MOJO* from the lesson.

Year 2 Week 17b

Music magazines – media industries and media audiences

Learning objectives – learners will be able to:

- explain how the Bauer group are diversified over media forms and products
- outline how different Bauer products target different audiences
- suggest the uses and gratifications offered by *MOJO*
- explain different possible audience interpretations of *MOJO*.

Key products

Centres need at least two magazines so that learners can study one whole edition and at least two covers.

MOJO **magazine**

Music magazine alternative

Bauer Media Group (http://www.bauermedia.co.uk/)

MOJO **magazine homepage** (http://www.mojo4music.com/)

Additional resources

Bauer Media Group, Our Company (http://www.bauermedia.co.uk/about/our-company), **Culture & Values** (http://www.bauermedia.co.uk/about/culture-values)

IPSO (https://www.ipso.co.uk/about-ipso/who-ipso-regulates/?letters=m)

Teacher activities

- Direct a whole-class discussion on the uses and gratifications offered by magazines (and specifically *MOJO*) and the role of gender, age and fandom.
- Direct a whole-class discussion on different possible audience interpretations of *MOJO*, encouraging learners to try out and apply key terms.
- Check that learners' magazine funding research includes notes on the lack of regulation for print media (e.g. due to ideals of 'press freedom', *MOJO* has joined IPSO as the regulator run by the newspaper and magazine industry).

Learner activities

- As a class, learners discuss the uses and gratifications offered by magazines and audience interpretations of *MOJO*.
- Learners research the Bauer group range of brands and their audience reach (in terms of age and gender categories), focusing on magazine funding, circulation, advertising, events, etc.
- Learners feed back their research on the Bauer group to the whole class.

Suggested homework

Learners write an essay: 'How are the music magazines you have studied regulated and identify their target audience.'

Year 2 Week 18a

Print news – genre and newspapers

Learning objectives – learners will be able to:

- state the generic conventions of 'quality' and 'tabloid' newspapers.

Key products

Print copies of the front pages of two quality and two tabloid newspapers, e.g. *The Sun, The Mirror, The Observer, The Daily Telegraph*

Teacher activities

- Review key elements of print media language.
- Ask learners to work in pairs to analyse one pair of quality and tabloid newspapers and note the key differences in terms of layout, typography, use of images and language and content.
- Get pairs to share their analysis with another pair and decide on a list of generic conventions summarising the differences between the tabloid and quality newspapers.
- Facilitate whole-class feedback.
- Explain the more male and working-class audience for tabloids, more mixed-gender and middle-class audience for the qualities.
- Direct a whole-class discussion on genre and uses and gratifications.

Learner activities

- In pairs, learners analyse one pair of quality and tabloid newspapers and note the key differences in terms of layout, typography, use of images and language and content.
- In fours, learners share analyses and check the other pair's analysis against the product. They decide on a list of generic conventions summarising the differences between the tabloid and quality newspapers.
- Learners share their conventions with the rest of the class and the class decides on the final set of generic conventions.
- Learners discuss the different uses and gratifications offered by tabloid and quality newspapers (e.g. importance of information or entertainment, identification with the values of the newspaper and a sense of belonging, offering stories or issues to share with others).

Year 2 Week 18b

News – political influence and regulation

Learning objectives – learners will be able to:

- discuss the political influence of print newspapers and their political leanings
- outline political debates about the regulation of print newspapers.

Key products

Print copies of the front pages of politically opposing tabloid and quality newspapers covering a big political story (preferably but not necessarily Sunday editions), e.g. *The Sun, The Mirror, The Observer, The Telegraph*

Or online coverage of opposing front pages on election day (http://www.pressgazette.co.uk/sun-warns-of-apocalypse-if-labour-wins-as-telegraph-express-and-daily-mail-also-give-may-front-page-polling-day-support/)

BBC News guide to the regulation issues that led to the Leveson Inquiry (http://www.bbc.co.uk/news/uk-15686679)

Teacher activities

- Review genre conventions of quality and tabloid newspapers.
- Lead whole-class discussion of the context for the political event covered in the newspapers.
- Ask learners to work in pairs to note the political differences between the newspapers.
- Explain how the political role of newspapers in criticising or supporting political parties and commenting on policies depends on their freedom from the PSB requirement to be impartial, hence the demand for a free press not to be regulated or controlled by the state. Facilitate a class discussion on ways in which state control of the press can be used by dictators (e.g. by denying any opposition a voice and rigging elections).
- Provide learners with the BBC article about the Leveson Inquiry for them to read.
- Facilitate a class discussion. Should the press be regulated to prevent invasion of privacy and corruption of the police, or is the freedom of the press more important?

Learner activities

- In pairs, learners note the political differences between the front-page coverage of the newspapers.
- Learners read the summary of the Leveson Inquiry and, as a class, discuss the issue of press regulation.

Suggested homework

Learners research press freedom around the world using https://rsf.org/en/ranking#.

Year 2 Week 19a

News – newspaper media industries

> ### Learning objectives – learners will be able to:
>
> - identify the sources of funding for newspapers
> - identify IPSO and IMPRESS as two competing self-regulators
> - explain the difficulties faced by newspapers due to declining circulation and advertising revenue following competition from the internet.

Key products

Articles about:

Declining circulation figures for newspapers (https://en.wikipedia.org/wiki/List_of_newspapers_in_the_United_Kingdom_by_circulation)

Declining print advertising revenue (https://www.wsj.com/articles/plummeting-newspaper-ad-revenue-sparks-new-wave-of-changes-1476955801)

Failure of digital revenue to make up for loss of print revenue (http://uk.businessinsider.com/statistics-smartphones-print-newspaper-revenues-2017-2)

Teacher activities

- Outline traditional sources of funding for newspapers: circulation (cover price) and classified and display advertising.
- Outline newer sources of funding: online paywalls, innovative forms of advertising such as native content and sponsored content, membership, events (e.g. *Guardian* talks and courses) and sales (e.g. travel, books).
- Review the Leveson recommendation for newspaper self-regulation to be checked by an independent body to ensure that standards are met. Outline how IMPRESS (Leveson-compliant) and IPSO (not Leveson-compliant) are rival self-regulators.
- Distribute circulation figures and direct discussion on why print newspapers are declining.
- Distribute information about falling advertising revenue and direct a class discussion on what we will lose if newspapers go out of business.

Learner activities

- Working in small groups, learners note which, if any, newspapers are read at home and whether anyone in the group would be willing to pay for news content. They note which sources of news the group has used in the last week. They share with the rest of the class and decide the number one reason for not buying a newspaper.
- As a class, learners discuss the importance of newspapers. What are the possible advantages of having our news chosen for us by professionals rather than by algorithms on Facebook?

Year 2 Week 19b

News – newspaper media industries

Learning objectives – learners will be able to:

- state an example of online newspapers' paywalls
- state the global reach of online versions of newspapers
- identify online-only newspapers such as *BuzzFeed*
- explain why online-only newspapers are not regulated.

Key products

Access to online newspapers, e.g. *The Telegraph* or *The Times/Sunday Times* for examples of paywalls, *BuzzFeed* or *The Independent* for an example of online-only

Data on online newspapers (e.g. http://www.stateofthemedia.org/2013/newspapers-stabilizing-but-still-threatened/19-top-10-online-newspapers-worldwide/)

Teacher activities

- Review issue of monetising online content. Display or ask learners to access at least one online newspaper with a paywall and note the charge for content.
- Display the number of unique users for *The Guardian* (120 million per month in 2017) and the *Mail* online (240 million per month in 2017) and direct discussion on why newspapers without paywalls are more successful.
- Display an example of an online newspaper or ask students to access at least one example.
- Direct discussion on why newspapers such as *BuzzFeed* are not part of IPSO, even though the head of IPSO has expressed the desire that they should be (the ideals of freedom and unfettered innovation on the web, the international nature of online newspapers, the political debate about the power of the press still mostly considering print journalism, etc.).

Learner activities

- Learners note one example of an online newspaper paywall.
- As a class, learners discuss what, if anything, they would be willing to pay for news content. What services are they willing to pay for on the internet?
- Learners note how the online-only newspaper differs from the online *Observer*.
- As a class, learners discuss the difficulties of regulating online news content (including 'fake news').

Suggested homework

Learners research and note any differences between British newspapers and an online version of an American newspaper, e.g. *The New York Times.*

Year 2 Week 20a

News – media ownership: *The Observer*

> ### Learning objectives – learners will be able to:
> ● outline the effects of the ownership of the GMG by the Scott Trust
> ● explain *The Guardian/Observer*'s social and political ethos.

Key products

Explanation of the role of the Scott Trust (https://www.theguardian.com/membership/2016/oct/24/scott-trust-guardian-owner-journalism-newspaper – see the one-minute embedded video for a summary)

Article explaining *The Guardian* to an American readership and covering *Guardian* scoops on Snowden, Manning and phone hacking (https://www.theatlantic.com/national/archive/2013/07/how-i-the-guardian-i-broke-the-snowden-story/277486/ – could be edited down slightly)

***Guardian* stories about Snowden** (e.g. https://www.businessinsider.com.au/guardian-editor-says-british-intelligence-agents-destroyed-their-hard-drives-2013-8 – print front page; https://www.theguardian.com/world/2013/sep/05/nsa-gchq-encryption-codes-security; https://www.theguardian.com/world/2013/jun/30/nsa-leaks-us-bugging-european-allies)

Teacher activities

● Screen the video about the Scott Trust and note and explain the key values espoused: 'open, honest, acting with integrity, courage and fairness, liberal progressive values'.
● Direct class discussion of how far these are values that any newspaper would espouse and how far these are specific to *The Guardian/Observer*.
● Distribute the article from *The Atlantic*, explaining the Snowden revelations, the phone hacking scandal (including Milly Dowler) and the issues of civil liberties raised by these cases.

Learner activities

● Learners read the article from *The Atlantic*.
● As a class, learners discuss how these *Guardian/Observer* scoops fit their belief in 'liberal, progressive' values, using *The Guardian* headlines on Snowden as an example.

Suggested homework

Learners write an essay: 'How do newspapers reflect the media industries that own them? Use *The Observer* as an example.'

Year 2 Week 20b

News – audience: *The Observer*

Learning objectives – learners will be able to:

- state *The Observer*'s target audience: progressive, educated, middle class, mixed gender
- identify that *The Guardian/Observer* have chosen not to place online content behind a paywall but ask for voluntary membership to fund the newspaper in an era of declining sales
- discuss the uses and gratifications offered by such a membership model.

Key products

The Observer print front pages

Online *Observer* homepage (https://www.theguardian.com/observer)

Teacher activities

- Review *The Observer* target audience material from Year 1.
- Ask learners, in pairs or small groups, to look for evidence on the homepage and print front pages of *The Observer* of it addressing its target audience in terms of content and style.
- Direct whole-class discussion on learners' findings.
- Review the uses and gratifications theory.
- Ask learners, in pairs or small groups, to read the footer on the online *Observer* pages asking for membership and justifying this approach to funding online news, and suggest how this approach rather than a paywall might offer uses and gratifications to the audience.
- Direct whole-class discussion on learners' suggestions.

Learner activities

- In pairs/small groups, learners look for evidence on the homepage and print front pages of *The Observer* of it addressing its target audience in terms of content and style.
- In pairs/small groups, learners read the footer on the online *Observer* pages asking for membership and justifying this approach to funding online news. They suggest how this approach rather than a paywall might offer uses and gratifications to the audience.

Year 2 Week 21a

News – print media language

Learning objectives – learners will be able to:

- analyse two *Observer* front covers in terms of layout, typography, language use, images, graphics and colour
- identify key elements of *The Observer* house style
- state how *The Observer* uses the advantages of print technology on its front page
- identify any use of intertextuality on the front pages.

Key products

Class set of front pages of two editions of *The Observer* dating from after the start of the course

Class set of one complete edition of *The Observer* dating from after the start of the course

Images of other Sunday newspaper front pages for comparison

Teacher activities

- Run a review activity for the elements of print media language.
- Organise learners into pairs. Each pair takes one media language element and notes continuities in the two front pages and the connotations of this media language. They share their findings with the rest of the group to create a complete analysis.
- Direct whole-class discussion of house style, displaying other front pages to illustrate what is specific about *The Observer*'s style.
- Set 'advantages of print' task, facilitate, run plenary.

Learner activities

- In pairs, learners take one media language element and note continuities in the two front pages and the connotations of this media language. They share their findings with the rest of the group to create a complete analysis.
- Learners explore inside the newspaper for changes and continuities in media language in different sections. They decide on the key elements of *The Observer* house style and collect at least one example of intertextuality.
- In pairs, learners discuss the advantages of print technology – the ability to produce lengthy and detailed copy and to use layout for impact (e.g. headlines, large images), the sense of occasion afforded by a printed product.
- Pairs feed back to the class.
- Lead a class discussion: 'Would you rather read a printed newspaper or the online version?'

Suggested homework

Pick one other quality newspaper (e.g. *Sunday Telegraph* or *Sunday Times*) and note how its front page differs in media language from *The Observer.*

Year 2 Week 21b

News – representation

Learning objectives – learners will be able to:

- analyse representations in two front covers of *The Observer*.

Key products

Front covers of two editions of *The Observer* dating from after the start of the course

Images of other Sunday newspaper front pages for comparison

Teacher activities

- Direct whole-class discussion about presence and absence of social groups in *The Observer*.
- Organise learners into pairs and ask them to discuss the use of stereotypes (and/or anti-stereotypes) in *The Observer* – especially gender stereotypes.
- Facilitate feedback and class discussion of learners' findings.
- Direct whole-class discussion about messages and values, using contrasting front pages to foreground *The Observer*'s view of the world.

Learner activities

- As a class, learners analyse the social groups present in and absent from *The Observer* and discuss the reasons for this presence/absence.
- In pairs, learners discuss the use of stereotypes (and/or anti-stereotypes) in *The Observer* – especially gender stereotypes.
- Pairs feed back their findings to the class.
- As a class, learners analyse the messages and values in *The Observer* and consider what view of the world the front pages construct.

Year 2 Week 22a

News – media language in historical products

> ### Learning objectives – learners will be able to:
>
> - analyse how the media language style in the three historical *Observer* front covers differs from the contemporary editions.

Key products

A class set of the three set front covers of historical editions of *The Observer* dating from 1966–68: these will be made available on the OCR website. They are also available from 'ProQuest' (log-in required, may be available from libraries)

Contemporary *Observer* front pages for comparison

Teacher activities

- Reassure students that the Media Studies exam does not require them to memorise the differences in the content between the three historical front pages (or their dates of publication), just the main differences in media language style from the contemporary editions.
- Set an activity to review the media language analysis of the contemporary *Observer* from last week.
- Group learners into pairs and ask them to read the three front pages and analyse the key differences in media language between contemporary and historical editions.
- Facilitate feedback of pairs' findings to the class and whole-class discussion.
- Explain differences in technology between contemporary and 1960s newspapers.

Learner activities

- In pairs, learners read the three front pages and analyse the key differences in media language between contemporary and historical editions, e.g. monochrome versus colour, fewer stories on the front page and greater use of images in the contemporary editions, less formal language used in the contemporary editions (e.g. in how politicians are named), greater use of marketing on the front pages in the contemporary editions, more cluttered, 'newsy' layout in the historical editions.
- Pairs feed back their findings to the group and learners discuss them as a class.

Suggested homework

Learners look online at images of other 1960s newspapers.

Year 2 Week 22b

News – representation in historical products

Learning objectives – learners will be able to:

● analyse differences in representations in news stories in the three historical *Observer* front covers from the contemporary editions.

Key products

Three set front covers of historical editions of *The Observer* dating from 1966–68 – these will be made available on the OCR website, they are also available from ProQuest (log-in required, may be available from libraries)

Teacher activities

● Reassure students that the Media Studies exam does not require them to memorise the differences in the representations between the three historical front pages (or their dates of publication), just examples of news stories across the three front pages that illustrate representations.

● Review the representation analysis of the contemporary *Observer* from last week.

● Group learners into pairs and ask them to note key aspects of the representations in the historical editions of *The Observer* that differ from those common today.

● Facilitate feedback of pairs' findings to the class and whole-class discussion.

● Direct whole-class discussion on continuities in representations.

Learner activities

● In pairs, learners note key aspects of the representations in the historical editions that differ from those common today, e.g. the mention of equal pay for women as not yet attainable and the article suggesting that a 'mixed-race' marriage was news; the emphasis on strikes and industrial relations.

● As a class, learners analyse continuities in representation, e.g. concerns over Europe and Russia.

Suggested homework

Learners discuss with people in their 60s and older what life was like in the 1960s.

Year 2 Week 23a

News – contexts and the print *Observer*

> ### Learning objectives – learners will be able to:
>
> - describe and exemplify the changes in how media contexts influence representations in the contemporary and historical editions of *The Observer.*

Key products

Three set front covers of historical editions of *The Observer* dating from 1966–68 – these will be made available on the OCR website, they are also available from ProQuest (log-in required, may be available from libraries)

Class sets of contemporary front covers of *The Observer*

Teacher activities

- Review the representation and media language analysis of the historical *Observer* from last week.
- Review the meaning of 'social, cultural, political and historical contexts', emphasising that these may overlap, especially the social and cultural, and that the social, cultural and political contexts may be either historical or contemporary. Remind learners of the contexts of the representations in *The Avengers*.
- Ask learners to work in pairs to note examples from the historical front covers of *The Observer* that reflect the cultural attitudes and historical context of mid-1960s Britain.
- Run whole-class discussions on how this is similar to the Britain represented in *The Avengers* and how it differs from the Britain represented in the contemporary *Observer*.

Learner activities

- In pairs, learners note examples from the historical front covers of *The Observer* that reflect that mid-1960s Britain was dominated by white males, had very few women in positions of power, saw 'race' from a white point of view as about non-white people who are 'different', assumed heterosexuality to be 'normal', worried about whether it should join 'Europe', the Russian threat, strikes, and whether it should allow social reforms, e.g. to make male gay sex legal and to allow women to divorce more easily and have abortions.
- As a class, learners discuss how this is similar to the Britain represented in *The Avengers*.
- As a class, learners discuss the ways this differs from the Britain represented in the contemporary *Observer*.

Year 2 Week 23b

News – contexts and the print *Observer*

Learning objectives – learners will be able to:

- describe and exemplify the changes in how media contexts influence the media language in the contemporary and historical editions of *The Observer*
- describe and exemplify the continuities in how media contexts influence contemporary and historical editions of *The Observer*.

Key products

Three set front covers of historical editions of *The Observer* dating from 1966–68 – these will be made available on the OCR website, they are also available from ProQuest (log-in required, may be available from libraries)

Class sets of contemporary front covers of *The Observer*

Teacher activities

- Review the work on contexts and representations from the previous lesson.
- Ask learners to work in pairs to analyse the influence of contexts on the media language of contemporary newspapers when compared with those from the 1960s.
- Facilitate feedback to the class and class discussion.
- Explain the continuities in the historical contexts that influence the historical and contemporary newspapers in similar ways: the threat to Europe from its large neighbour Russia, debates about Britain's role in the world – should it remain separate or become European?
- Lead class discussion exploring continuities in the influence of cultural contexts on what counts as news (news values), e.g. bad news, news of culturally important places or people.

Learner activities

- In pairs, learners analyse the influence of contexts on the media language of contemporary newspapers when compared with those from the 1960s: improved technology, a less deferential society (less politeness to 'superiors') and a consumerist society dominated by marketing and offering 'consumer choice'.
- In small groups, learners pick out examples from historical and contemporary front pages of continuities in representation that reflect contexts, e.g. concerns over Europe and Russia, what counts as news.

Suggested homework

Learners write an essay: 'How do newspapers reflect the historical, social and cultural contexts in which they are produced? Refer to *The Observer* in your answer.'

Year 2 Week 24a

Online news – media language and contexts

Learning objectives – learners will be able to:

- analyse the homepage and at least one other page in terms of layout, typography, images, graphics, language use, colour, links and embedded audio-visual material
- discuss how the *Observer* house style reflects the ethos of the newspaper
- discuss how the *Observer* house style reflects the generic conventions of a 'quality' newspaper
- identify the influence of media contexts on the media language of the online newspaper.

Key product

The Observer website (a different edition from that analysed in the first year): https://www.theguardian.com/observer

Teacher activities

- Review the generic conventions of a 'quality' newspaper and the ethos of *The Guardian/Observer*.
- Organise learners into groups of eight, working as four pairs. Each analyses one of: (1) layout and typography; (2) images, graphics and colour; (3) language use; (4) links and embedded audio-visual material. Pairs add their analyses to those of the other pairs for each element.
- Direct a whole-class review of the key elements of the house style established last year by listing differences and continuities between the homepage and other pages on the website, reviewing how far this fits the generic conventions of 'quality' newspapers and the liberal ethos of *The Guardian/Observer*.
- Ask learners to work in pairs to list the media language elements they would expect to find on any good website.
- Direct class discussion of the cultural expectations of the media language of websites when compared with print products (e.g. immediacy and choice, ease of access, simplicity of layout, hypertext, signalling opportunities for participation) and to what extent the homepage meets these expectations. Establish that these expectations form the cultural context for the website.

Learner activities

- Working in groups of eight, four pairs each analyse one of: (1) layout and typography; (2) images, graphics and colour; (3) language use; (4) links and embedded audio-visual material. Pairs add their analyses to those of the other pairs for each element.
- In pairs, learners list the media language elements they would expect to find on any good website.

Year 2 Week 24b

Online news – representations and contexts

Learning objectives – learners will be able to:

- analyse the representations on *The Observer* homepage
- discuss how these representations address *The Observer* target audience and reflect *The Observer*'s values and beliefs, especially in relation to inclusivity and avoiding stereotyping
- identify the influence of media contexts on the representations in the online newspaper.

Key product

***The Observer* website** (a different edition from that analysed in the first year): https://www.theguardian.com/observer

Teacher activities

- Review how the media language in *The Observer* fits generic conventions and the ethos of the newspaper.
- Review *The Guardian/Observer*'s target audience.
- Organise learners into groups of eight, working as four pairs. Each analyses representations of one of the following: (1) gender; (2) race/ethnicity; (3) nations/the world; (4) the assumed lifestyle of the audience. Pairs share their analyses with the rest of their group.
- Direct class discussion on the influence of contexts on representations (e.g. the influence of celebrity culture, of consumerism, of inequality, power and influence within Britain and the world, of cultural expectations of established newspapers, as relevant).

Learner activities

- Working in groups of eight, four pairs each analyse representations of one of the following: (1) gender; (2) race/ethnicity; (3) nations/the world; (4) the assumed lifestyle of the audience. Pairs then share their analyses with the rest of their group and list examples of addressing a liberal audience, e.g. by avoiding stereotyping and/or inclusive representation.

Suggested homework

Learners write an essay: 'To what extent is the online *Observer* a continuation of the print version?'

Year 2 Week 25a

News – use of social media: media language

Learning objectives – learners will be able to:

- analyse *The Guardian/Observer* Twitter and Instagram feed in terms of layout, typography, images, graphics, language use, colour, links and embedded audio-visual
- compare these with the house style of the website.

Key products

The Guardian **Instagram feed:** www.instagram.com/guardian/?hl=en

The Guardian **Twitter feed:** https://twitter.com/guardian

The Observer **staff Twitter feed:** https://twitter.com/guardian/lists/observer-staff?lang=en

Teacher activities

- Review the media language analysis from Weeks 17 and 18 last year.
- Ask learners to work in pairs to analyse either *The Guardian* Instagram feed or Twitter feed and compare it with *The Observer* staff Twitter feed.
- Direct discussion on how far the media language in Twitter and Instagram feeds is determined by the newspaper or by the social media site.
- Review *The Observer* website house style analysis from the previous lesson and direct class discussion on the key elements of similarity and difference between the website and the social media feeds.

Learner activities

- In pairs, learners analyse the media language in either *The Guardian* Instagram feed or the Twitter feed and compare it with the other *Observer* Instagram or Twitter feed.
- Learners take part in a whole-class discussion on the key elements of similarity and difference between the website and the social media feeds.

Year 2 Week 25b

Online news and social media – representation and audience participation

Learning objectives – learners will be able to:

- compare representations in *The Guardian/Observer* Twitter feed and Instagram feed with those on the website
- discuss opportunities for the audience to participate in discussions on social media and the 'Comment is free' pages of *The Guardian* website
- cite examples of different audience interpretations of articles.

Key products

The Guardian **Instagram feed:** http://www.instagram.com/guardian/?hl=en

The Guardian **Twitter feed:** https://twitter.com/guardian

The Guardian **'Comment is free' pages:** http://www.theguardian.com/uk/commentisfree

Teacher activities

- Review the representation analysis from last year.
- Set the representation task and facilitate and run the plenary (discussing whether the importance of the image on Instagram creates different 'news values' and whether the similarities between a newspaper tweet and a headline make the Twitter feed more like the online newspaper).
- Explain to learners that *The Guardian* and *The Observer* are both owned by the Guardian Media Group, which in turn is owned by Scott Trust Limited. The two newspapers target similar audiences. The strong links between the two newspapers mean that their Twitter and Instagram feeds are shared.
- Review the concepts of audience activity and passivity.
- Set the audience participation task and facilitate and run the plenary (discussing to what extent the audience are truly active on these feeds or simply reacting to the agenda set by the newspaper).

Learner activities

- In pairs, learners analyse the representations in *The Guardian* Instagram and Twitter feeds and note the similarities and differences from the representations in *The Observer* website.
- Learners note one example of an article in the 'Comment is free' pages of *The Guardian* that generates a large audience debate (they note the headline and the substance of at least two comments: one that agrees and one that disagrees with the author of the article). They note any differences in types of audience response between 'Comment is free' and the Twitter and Instagram feeds.

Suggested homework

Learners make notes on the differences between the Twitter and Instagram feeds of a celebrity and those of the newspaper.

Year 2 Week 28a

Revision and exam practice – media language

Learning objectives – learners will be able to:

- recall media language terminology from previous sessions
- practise denotation and connotation examples using media language
- analyse the ways in which media producers use media language to create meanings for audiences.

Key products

Centres need at least two magazines so that learners can study one whole edition and at least two covers.

MOJO magazine

Music magazine alternative

Use any other relevant key products to help revision and exam practice, such as **MOJO magazine homepage** (http://www.mojo4music.com/).

Teacher activities

- Give learners a list of key terms and their definitions for media language.
- Recap (perhaps using a brief quiz) the key terms of magazine media language.
- Give learners definitions of denotation and connotation.
- Ask learners to list examples of denotation and connotation. Reinforce the terms 'generic codes and conventions'. Explain that producers target different audiences through their use of media language.
- Direct whole-class discussion on the uses and gratifications theory, encouraging learners to try out and apply the key terms.

Learner activities

- Learners check their recall and understanding of media language.
- As a class, learners discuss denotation and connotation, learning to apply the correct terminology.
- Using computers, learners work in pairs to research the uses and gratifications theory and discuss how it can be applied to different magazines. It may be helpful to give learners a list of questions to aid their research.
- Learners contribute to class feedback using the notes they have made.

Suggested homework

Learners write up their notes on denotation/connotation and the uses and gratifications theory from the lesson and research further music magazine examples.

Year 2 Week 28b

Revision and exam practice – media language

Learning objectives – learners will be able to:

- analyse *MOJO* magazine and *UNCUT* magazine front covers in terms of media language (e.g. layout, typography, image, graphics, colour and language use)
- repeat and practise media language terminology.

Key products

Centres need at least two magazines so that learners can study one whole edition and at least two covers.

MOJO magazine

Music magazine alternative

MOJO **magazine homepage** (http://www.mojo4music.com/)

UNCUT **magazine homepage** (http://www.uncut.co.uk/)

Use any other relevant key products to help revision and exam practice.

Teacher activities

- Recap denotation and connotation notes and the uses and gratifications theory from the previous session. Perhaps a brief quiz could be used.
- Display *MOJO* magazine and one other unseen music magazine (e.g. *UNCUT*), directing learners, in pairs, to complete a comparison analysis of media language.
- Facilitate student feedback.
- Set the timed writing task (15 minutes) for learners to complete: 'How far is media language used differently on *MOJO* magazine and *UNCUT* magazine front covers to reflect genre conventions?'

Learner activities

- Learners share their notes on denotation/connotation and the uses and gratifications theory from the previous lesson.
- As a class, learners discuss denotation/connotation and the uses and gratifications theory, learning to apply the correct terminology.
- In pairs, learners compare and analyse the media language used in the magazines. They feed back their analysis to the class.
- Learners complete the timed writing activity. They should analyse examples of how media language is used similarly and differently. They should also make judgements and reach conclusions about whether there are more similarities due to genre conventions than differences.

Suggested homework

Learners revise denotation/connotation, the uses and gratifications theory and media language of *MOJO* magazine and other music magazines.

Year 2 Week 29a

Revision – television

Learning objectives – learners will be able to:

- make notes under timed conditions
- identify key media terminology from key sequences.

Key products

The Avengers, Series 4, Episode 1, ITV

Cuffs, Series 1, Episode 1, BBC1

Teacher activities

- Introduce methods of taking notes under timed conditions; talk through different approaches (bullet points, spider-diagram, grids, etc.).
- Screen twice a key sequence of approximately five minutes from *The Avengers*, with a break of two minutes between screenings.
- Direct learners to practise note-making using one method, focusing on how one area of media language (camerawork, editing, mise-en-scène or sound) creates effects in the sequence.
- Facilitate feedback from learners on how effective they felt their method was.
- Screen twice a key sequence from *Cuffs* of approximately five minutes, with a break of two minutes between screenings.
- Direct learners to practise a second method of note-taking, focusing on a different area of media language and how it creates effects in the sequence.
- Ask learners to write up their analysis of how their chosen area of media language creates effects in the sequence, under timed conditions (approximately 10 minutes).
- Direct learners to peer review another learner's writing.

Learner activities

- Learners make notes on one area of media language (camerawork, editing, mise-en-scène or sound) in *The Avengers* under timed conditions.
- Learners feed back one strength and one weakness of their chosen note-taking method.
- Learners make a second set of notes on an area of media language in *Cuffs*.
- They feed back one strength and one weakness of their second chosen note-taking method.
- Learners write up one analysis.
- Learners peer review one analysis, identifying strengths and weaknesses of the writing, focusing on use of media language terms and connotations.

Year 2 Week 29b

Revision – television

Learning objectives – learners will be able to:

- compare and contrast representations found in *Cuffs* and *The Avengers*
- compare and contrast narrative and genre in the crime and spy genres.

Key products

The Avengers, Series 4, Episode 1, ITV

Cuffs, Series 1, Episode 1, BBC1

Teacher activities

- Recap exam structure and requirements, including the number of questions on the exam paper and allocated marks.
- Organise learners into small groups. Ask them to refer to their notes.
- Give each group a different area to revise, including representations found within the texts, how narrative is formed within the programmes and any contrasts that can be drawn, differences and similarities between the spy and crime genres, audience appeal (including uses and gratifications theory) and a comparison of the scheduling for each programme. Structured questions will aid this activity.
- Each group must produce a revision handout which covers the main elements. This could be a word document or similar-sized hand-written document
- Facilitate feedback.

Learner activities

- In small groups, learners use their notes to produce a revision handout for one area. It will be shared with the rest of the class to form a large revision booklet.

Suggested homework

Learners revise media contexts for both television products.

Year 2 Week 30a

Revision and exam practice – promoting media (film)

Learning objectives – learners will be able to:

- recall media industries terms and definitions
- analyse the ways in which regulation supports media industries
- understand the benefits of synergy within the film industry.

Key products

The Lego Movie film

The Lego Movie video game

Teacher activities

- Conduct a brief test to secure understanding of key media industries terms.
- Display (or provide the logos of) the range of regulatory bodies studied.
- Check that learners have the correct definitions recorded.
- Ask learners to work on the impact that an absence of regulation could have on the industry.
- Provide a sample 4-mark question for learners to test their knowledge of the benefits for film companies of linking films and video games.
- Ask learners to reflect beyond the financial benefits of companies linking their products to films.

Learner activities

- Learners define key media industries terms, showing understanding of media language.
- In pairs, learners recap and discuss the roles of regulatory bodies.
- In groups, learners discuss the role of regulation in the film and video game industries.
- Learners write a practice answer.
- In groups, learners discuss and collate a list of reasons for linking films and video games.

Suggested homework

Learners produce their own revision sheet focusing on industry regulatory bodies and their role.

Year 2 Week 30b

Revision and exam practice – promoting media (film)

Learning objectives – learners will be able to:

- analyse and apply genre codes
- recall Blumler and Katz's uses and gratifications theory in relation to video games.

Key products

The Lego Movie **UK TV trailer:** https://www.youtube.com/watch?v=Yj4GeCk5SBk

The Lego Movie **poster campaign:** http://www.impawards.com/2014/lego_movie_gallery.html

Teacher activities

- Recap representation. Divide students into groups and ask them to reflect on an area of representation in *The Lego Movie* trailer. Facilitate feedback.
- Direct a group discussion that highlights examples of intertextuality within *The Lego Movie* poster campaign.
- Recap media language and ask pairs to reflect on the genre codes and conventions within the trailer and poster campaign.
- Ask learners to recall as much as they can from Blumler and Katz's uses and gratifications theory in five minutes.
- Set the timed writing task for homework.

Learner activities

- In groups, learners log examples of their allocated representational issue in *The Lego Movie* trailer. They prepare to feed back to the rest of the class.
- As a class, learners discuss intertextuality.
- In pairs, learners identify genre codes and conventions in *The Lego Movie* advertising. How far does the media form dictate these codes?
- Individually, learners note down their knowledge of the uses and gratifications theory.

Suggested homework

Learners write a timed model answer to the following question: 'How does *The Lego Movie* video game provide uses and gratifications to its audience? Refer to Blumler and Katz's theory in your answer' (10 minutes).

Year 2 Week 31a

Revision – active and passive audiences

Learning objectives – learners will be able to:

- apply the concepts of active and passive audiences across a range of media forms.

Key products

Cuffs

The Avengers

The Lego Movie advertising

The Lego Movie video game

MOJO magazine

Set music videos

Radio 1 *Live Lounge*

The Observer online

Teacher activities

- Direct whole-group discussion to list the different ways audiences can be active, e.g. user-generated content, generating narrative events, reacting with likes, comments, retweets and so on, discussing media content while watching (e.g. second screening), choosing between multiple options. Review the concept of audience passivity. Is passivity always a bad thing?
- Ask learners to work in pairs and list ways audiences can be active for each of the media forms for which audience is studied. Run a plenary, adding forms of activity not previously listed.
- Ask learners to work in small groups to rank the above media forms in terms of the degree of audience activity they allow. Explain that there is no right answer to this task and that they will not be asked to do this in the exam – it is to help them think about the media form as a whole.
- Direct whole-group discussion: how does audience activity affect the uses and gratifications offered by a media form?

Learner activities

- In pairs, learners list ways audiences can be active for each of the media forms for which audience is studied: TV, advertising, video games, music videos, radio, online.
- In small groups, learners rank the above media forms in terms of the degree of audience activity they allow.

Suggested homework

Learners revise for the whole exam.

Year 2 Week 31b

Revision – practice: unseen textual analysis

Learning objectives – learners will be able to:

- explain key elements of media industries for newspapers
- analyse unseen print and online newspapers in terms of media language and representation.

Key products

Unseen front cover of the print *Observer* and the online *Observer* homepage

Teacher activities

- Set a media industries quiz for newspapers (regulation, ownership, convergence, funding).
- Explain the key terms used in questions, especially that:
  - 'areas of the theoretical framework' means 'media language, audience, representations and industries'
  - 'make judgements and reach conclusions' means that learners have to weigh up arguments in answering the question (which will often be a 'how far' question), perhaps in a separate conclusion at the end of the answer which starts with the phrase 'In conclusion'.
- Set two practice media language and representation analyses; then run a plenary sharing key points of analysis:
  - one on print or online versions of *The Observer* about representation or media language (5 marks)
  - one on *The Observer* online, to be synoptic and include making judgements and reaching conclusions (15 marks).

Learner activities

- Learners complete the quiz and share answers.
- Learners answer analysis questions, e.g.:
  - Analyse the representations in the print *Observer* front page. Give two examples from the extract (5 marks).
  - How far is the media language of *The Observer* homepage due to its audience? In your answer, you should analyse the media language of the homepage, then make judgements and reach conclusions about whether the media language is due to the target audience or any other area of the theoretical framework (15 marks).

Suggested homework

Learners revise for the whole exam.

Year 2 Week 32a

Revision – television and contexts

Learning objectives – learners will be able to:

- compare *Cuffs* and *The Avengers* in relation to contexts.

Key products

Cuffs* and *The Avengers

Teacher activities

- Review the range of contexts: social, cultural, political and historical. Explain that the historical context is taken care of by the comparison between programmes from different time periods and that political contexts are not needed for television.
- Direct class revision on the influence of contexts on *Cuffs* and *The Avengers*.
- Set the practice essay and mark it for the next lesson.

Learner activities

- Learners complete a practice exam essay: 'Explain how social and cultural contexts influence television programmes. Refer to *The Avengers* and *Cuffs* to support your answer' (10 marks).
- Learners share their answer with one other learner to compare approaches to answering the question.

Suggested homework

Learners revise for the whole exam.

Year 2 Week 32b

Revision – newspapers and historical context

> ### Learning objectives – learners will be able to:
>
> - compare contemporary and historical editions of *The Observer* in relation to contexts.

Key products

Contemporary and historical editions of *The Observer*

Teacher activities

- Review the range of contexts: social, cultural, political and historical. Explain that political contexts are required for newspapers and that the historical is taken care of by comparison between newspapers from different time periods or from study of a historical newspaper.
- Direct class revision on the influence of contexts on contemporary and historical editions of *The Observer.*
- Set the practice essay.

Learner activities

- Learners complete a practice exam essay: 'Explain how the time and political contexts influence broadsheet newspapers. Refer to stories from a historical and contemporary edition of *The Observer* to support your answer' (10 marks).
- Learners share their answer with one other learner to compare approaches to answering the question.

Suggested homework

Learners revise for the whole exam.

Glossary

The terms below are listed in the OCR GCSE Media Studies specification as ones which learners are 'expected to know ... and how to comment on their use' (pp. 62–4 of the specification). These are followed by a list of other useful terms with which learners should be familiar.

Audio/visual

Camerawork

- establishing shots (long shots at the start of a scene establishing location and tone)
- low angle shots (looking up at the subject, e.g. 'worm's eye view')
- high angle shots (looking down on the subject)
- canted angle shots (or 'Dutch tilt' – camera tilted to one side to create diagonals)
- aerial shots ('bird's eye view' from above the subject)
- elaborate camera movement such as:
    - tracks (camera moves towards, away from or sideways alongside the subject)
    - steadicam (smooth hand-held camera movement, may flow around a scene)
    - crane shots (camera rises into the air, descends or swoops across a scene)
- hand-held camera (often creates juddering, urgent camerawork like a documentary)
- point-of-view shots (camera sees what a character sees, *not* over-the-shoulder shots)
- shallow focus and focus pulls (shallow focus means that one part of the shot is in focus and another isn't; a focus pull will change which part of the shot is in focus).

Editing

- shot/reverse shot (a cut between two characters showing both sides of an action including two characters, e.g. cutting from an over-the-shoulder shot of one character talking to an over-the-shoulder shot of the other character replying, reacting or listening)
- juxtaposition (creating extra meaning by placing one image next to another)
- non-continuity editing (e.g. deliberate jump cuts, where the subject jumps position in the frame in cutting from one shot to the next, usually due to the two shots being from the same angle)
- crosscutting (or 'parallel action' – cutting from one action in one location to another action in another location)
- fast-paced editing (short shots edited together rapidly)
- less common transitions: dissolve, wipe, fade
- post-production effects (e.g. visual effects added after filming).

Soundtrack

- music
- diegetic/non-diegetic sound (sound from within/from outside the fictional world; characters can 'hear' diegetic sound)
- sound effects (e.g. Foley effects added after filming – footsteps, weather sounds, gun shots, car engines and so on)
- sound bridge (where sound effects, music or recordings of ambient sound from one scene continue to the following one even though there is a cut to a different location; also used when the sound from the next scene is heard before we see the scene
- voiceover.

Mise-en-scène

- lighting, especially low-key lighting (low-key, or chiaroscuro, lighting creates dark shadows and extremes of light and shade)
- location/set

- costume and make-up
- props
- casting and performance style (the significance of casting may be explored by mentally replacing the actor with a different one; the performance style should be naturalistic in realistic dramas, for example)
- blocking (the composition of elements within the shot, especially the actors).

Print

Layout

- house style (repeated patterns of layout through a product)
- symmetrical and asymmetrical (balanced or unbalanced layout)
- use of columns and boxes
- ratio of copy (words), photography and space
- headline (heading at the top of a page or article)
- caption (a title or explanation of a photo or illustration)
- strapline (a subsidiary heading or caption)
- standfirst (brief summary of an article after the headline).

Typography

- serif and sans-serif typefaces (serif typefaces have ornaments or 'serifs', sans-serif don't)
- specialist typefaces (unusual typefaces)
- font size/italics/bold.

Language

- formal and informal register (language used to communicate impersonally and objectively; language used to communicate a shared relationship)
- direct mode of address (language addressing the person, e.g. by using the word 'you')
- puns, colloquialisms, slang.

Image

- graphics
- camerawork and mise-en-scène in photography
- depth of field (e.g. a shallow depth of field gives shallow focus)
- digital manipulation (e.g. photoshopping)
- cropping (removing parts of an image to improve composition or change meaning).

Colour

- house style (repeated use of the same colours throughout a publication)
- colour saturation (the intensity of a colour)
- choice of colour.

Online, social and participatory

Layout

- homepage (the start page on a website)
- navigation bar (a series of buttons or images with links to other pages of the website)
- tabs (markers for additional web pages that have been opened)
- house style (elements of layout repeated throughout a website).

Functionality

- roll-over (an element that changes when a cursor is rolled over it)
- pop-up (a smaller window that pops up onscreen)
- scrolling marquee (a scrolling area of text)
- links/hyperlinks (text or image that gives access to another text or image)
- embedded video/animations (video or animation in the web page)
- RSS feed (provides subscribers with new content from frequently updated websites)
- blog (a regularly updated informational or discussion website)
- interactivity (opportunities for audience feedback or user-generated content).

Typography

- branding (use of particular typefaces to represent the brand)
- specialist typefaces (unusual typefaces)
- font size/italics/bold.

Language

- formal and informal register (language used to communicate impersonally and objectively; language used to communicate a shared relationship)
- direct mode of address (language addressing the person, e.g. by using the word 'you').

Image

- graphics
- camerawork and mise-en-scène in photography
- depth of field (e.g. a shallow depth of field gives shallow focus)
- digital manipulation (e.g. photoshopping)
- cropping (removing parts of an image to improve composition or change meaning).

Colour

- house style (repeated use of the same colours throughout a website)
- choice of colour.

Other useful terms with which students should be familiar

- **active/passive audiences:** as a starting point, a useful explanation of the debates around audience reception theory can be found on BBC Bitesize at: http://www.bbc.co.uk/education/guides/zg24frd/revision/3. The concept of active audiences also includes users of online, social and participatory media
- **anti-stereotype:** a portrayal of a member of a social group, place, event or issue which goes against the generally accepted stereotype
- **blockbuster:** a film that is expected to have mass appeal and to be a big commercial success
- **causality:** cause and effect as part of the narrative structure
- **codes and conventions:** shared elements of a media product which are repeated so often that they become familiar
- **conglomerate:** a large (often multinational) business organisation which owns a number of different companies
- **connotation:** additional meanings and associations which can be interpreted from the detailed analysis of media products
- **contexts:** the social, cultural, historical and political context in which media products are produced and consumed
- **convergence:** the merging of previously separate media forms in one entity; for example, we use smartphones to take photographs, go online, watch films and television, stream music, etc.

Glossary

- **demographics:** a method of categorising audiences according to factual elements such as their job, income or status
- **denotation:** a description of what we see or hear in a media product
- **diversification:** when institutions branch out into other industries to limit risk
- **enigma:** a mystery which is presented to an audience and which helps to maintain their interest in the narrative
- **genre:** a category of media products which share codes and conventions and/or style, such as crime drama
- **globalisation:** the process by which institutions increasingly operate on a worldwide scale
- **hybrid:** a media product which combines a number of different genres
- **ideology:** a set of (usually shared) values and beliefs
- **interactivity:** where media products are created by or encourage the participation of the audience
- **intertextuality:** references to other media products which are expected to be recognised by the audience
- **mass/niche audiences:** large number of media users/media users with a special interest or of a specific demographic
- **media platform:** the way in which media content is delivered, such as smartphone, tablet, DVD, television, etc.
- **media product:** a text that has been designed to be consumed/used by an audience
- **mediation:** the process of interpreting, constructing and editing in order to represent a person, place, event or issue
- **mode of address:** the way in which a media product addresses or 'speaks' to its audience
- **narrative:** the way in which the story (factual or fictional) is told to the audience
- **patriarchy:** male dominance in society, supported by institutions
- **product placement:** when a product is advertised to the audience by being placed in a scene in a film or TV programme
- **prosumer:** the audience member who helps to create the media product through interactivity and participation (from a combination of consumer and producer)
- **psychographics:** a method of categorising audiences according to their values, attitudes and lifestyles
- **quality newspapers:** newspapers which cover mostly 'hard' or serious news stories, such as politics, business, foreign affairs. Quality newspapers in the UK are: *The Guardian, The Observer, The Times, The Sunday Times, The Daily Telegraph, The Sunday Telegraph, The Independent, The Financial Times.* These newspapers used to be referred to as 'broadsheets' until their formats were changed to 'compact', 'tabloid' or 'Berliner'
- **Reithian:** this refers to Lord Reith, first Director General of the BBC, who developed the first principles of public service broadcasting; in particular, that broadcasting should inform, educate and entertain
- **stereotype:** an over-simplified portrayal of a member of a social group, place, event or issue, which is based on assumptions
- **synergy:** where institutions work together to promote a product, to the benefit of both parties
- **theoretical framework:** media language, media representations, media industries, media audiences
- **uses and gratifications theory:** a useful explanation for learners of Blumler and Katz's theory can be found on BBC Bitesize at: http://www.bbc.co.uk/education/guides/zg24frd/revision/3
- **values:** a set of ideas and beliefs held by an individual, a group or the whole of society
- **vertical integration:** where a single company (or merged companies) controls both the production and the supply of a product